460960

W9-CKK-269

The Education of Jack Newfield

Also by Jack Newfield

A Prophetic Minority
Robert Kennedy: A Memoir
A Populist Manifesto, with Jeff Greenfield
Cruel and Unusual Justice
The Abuse of Power, with Paul DeBrul

The Education of Jack Newfield

JACK NEWFIELD

ST. MARTIN'S PRESS / NEW YORK

The articles in this book originally appeared in the *Village
Voice*, and are reprinted here with its permission. They
appeared in the following issues: August 11, 1975, June 17,
1981, September 14, 1982, May 3, 1983, September 24,
1979, March 3, 1980, December 6, 1976, October 17, 1977,
June 2, 1980, November 30, 1982, April 30, 1970, January
26, 1982, February 5, 1979, June 13, 1968, December 3,
1964, August 3, 1982, April 30, 1979, April 22, 1981, May
18, 1972.

Design by Mina Greenstein

Library of Congress Cataloging in Publication Data

Newfield, Jack.
    The education of Jack Newfield.

    I. Title.
PN4874.N37A25   1984   814'.54   83-21213
ISBN 0-312-23739-1

First Edition
10 9 8 7 6 5 4 3 2 1

Contents

Acknowledgments

Over twenty years a lot of people have contributed to my instruction. On this page, there are a special few I feel a need to acknowledge.

I have been enriched by the gift of community with fellow reporters. I have learned by watching them, listening to them, and reading them. I owe a special debt to: Murray Kempton, Nick Pileggi, Pete Hamill, Robert Caro, Gabe Pressman, Wayne Barrett, Syd Schanberg, Andrew Cooper, Seymour Hersh, Roger Wilkins, Nat Hentoff, I. F. Stone, Paul DeBrul, Joe Conason, and the late Carey McWilliams.

I have enjoyed the friendship of some extraordinary lawyers who have given me a free law school education in evidence, logic, doubt, public integrity, civil liberties, and justice. I thank Mario Cuomo, Joe Hynes, and Joe Bellacosa, all of St. John's Law School; Tom Puccio; Ed Korman; Victor Kovner; Bill Josephson; and Milton Mollen. They have been my personal Court of Appeals.

Ruth Messinger has been a friend, inspiration, and valued second opinion.

I have been lucky to have worked under a succession of *Voice* editors, each of whom has been splendid in a different way: Dan Wolf, Tom Morgan, Marianne Partridge, and David Schneiderman.

And most important of all has been my wife, Janie Eisenberg. Without her, none of this would be possible.

J.N.

Introduction

We all carry a variety of identities in our heads. I'm an only child and a poor kid from Bed-Stuy. I'm a graduate of a mostly black high school and of the City University—when it was still tuition-free. I'm a civil rights and antiwar activist from the 1960s, and a friend and biographer of Robert Kennedy. I'm a father and a husband; a democrat and a Jew; a muckraker and an empiricist. I cherish both Martin Luther King and Sugar Ray Robinson, so, please don't understand me too quickly.

My father died when I was four and my mother had to go to work to support us. I never went to summer camp or the country, and spent every July and August on the city streets. My origins and my affections are working class. My suspicion of authority is earned. And I have no liberal guilt because I had no advantages.

I grew up in Brooklyn during the 1950s, when we lost the *Eagle* and the Dodgers, so I grew accustomed to disappointment at an early age. Once, Pete Hamill and I, both native sons of Brooklyn, decided to simultaneously compose a list of "the three worst human beings of the twentieth century," and we each scrawled the same three names. Hitler, Stalin, and Walter O'Malley.

It's possible that the biggest influence on my becoming a liberal about race was Jackie Robinson. Seeing the vilification he took, and then watching him steal home or score from first on a single, affected me at least as much as reading *The Autobiography of Malcolm X*. Jackie Robinson's rookie year (1947) was my first lesson in equal opportunity and race discrimination—and I won't let myself forget it.

We all search for self-knowledge, and for some sustaining self-image that will save us from getting lost. I found my most precise and enduring self-image in 1968, when a friend named Fred Gardner gave me a copy of *The Autobiography of Lincoln Steffens* as a birthday present. In that volume is Steffens' description of his great mentor, Jacob Riis. I hope that when I am ninety, someone will write this about me.

"He [Jacob Riis] not only got the news; he cared about the news. He hated passionately all tyrannies, abuses, miseries, and he fought them. He was a 'terror' to the officials and landlords responsible, as he saw it, for the desperate condition of the tenements, where the poor lived. He had 'exposed' them in articles, books, and public speeches, and with results."

This disciple's description of Jacob Riis has ripened over time into my professional credo. I have cared about the news. I have hated passionately the overdogs who hurt tenants, or old people, or innocent citizens. And I have tried to get results, by going on radio and TV shows, and by confronting politicians and decision makers, and by sharing my files and information with other journalists. I did not expose the inhuman conditions in nursing homes just to document them for some future historian. My purpose was to improve those circumstances as soon as possible.

A second personal motto I have, which derives from my image of Jacob Riis, is that I should only try to be a "terror" with people bigger than me, and with institutions more influential than the *Village Voice*. Otherwise, journalism itself becomes the bully, as when "60 Minutes" chases one con man down an alley with a hand-held camera, or when all the media develops lynch mob psychology about someone who might actually be innocent—as in the case of Hamilton Jordan and the never-proven cocaine allegation against him.

Like Daniel Bell, I have come, in middle age, to think of myself as a radical in economics, a liberal in politics, and a conservative in culture.

By a radical in economics I mean that I want to democratize the current system, in which wealth purchases power in order to perpetuate wealth. I would like to see a redistribution of wealth in an egalitarian direction. This would also have the effect of diluting the concentration of power, which is now in too few hands. Money must be prevented from converting itself into privilege in the allocation of taxation, health care, housing, public office, education, and employment. In all these areas, *need* and *merit* should decide the distribution—not wealth or influence.

By a liberal in politics I mean that I believe in both individualism and pluralism; in electoral coalitions between the poor and the middle class; in racial equality; in the rule of law; and in the first ten amendments to the Constitution—all of them. And my favorite political writers are the bruised wise men of anti-Communism: Orwell, Milosz, Silone, Koestler, and Camus.

And by a conservative in culture I mean that I believe in tradition and continuity with the past; in the work ethic; in the family; and in the old-fashioned virtues inherent in education and morality. I am opposed to all "recreational" drugs; I have never tried cocaine. And I can only work on a manual typewriter.

My separation of these three realms, plus my strong bias for the particular, perhaps gives some of these pieces the appearance of incongruity or even paradox. But they do not, I hope, prove ultimately inconsistent at the level of values. I exposed a respected and philanthropic rabbi (Bernard Bergman) and was called "a typical self-hating Jew" by his furious friends. But a few years later I reflected on the world's indifference to anti-Semitism in an article that drew the most mail I've ever received.

I criticized special prosecutor Maurice Nadjari on civil liberties grounds, even though he was trying to convict the same politicians I was writing about in the *Village Voice*. He was abusing rights and employing unconstitutional shortcuts—means that did not justify the ends. Yet, a few years later I was one of the few journalists to defend the goals and methods of Abscam, while most left-of-center opinion makers found the government guilty of excess and misconduct.

In 1978 I wrote a piece arguing that Carol Bellamy, then the thirty-five-year-old president of New York's City Council, was a political hope for the future. By 1983, I had reconsidered. I thought she had lost touch with herself and her roots, and no longer knew who she was or what she really thought. So I contritely documented my second opinion.

But yes, there are a few underlying themes here. Character is more important than ideology. Integrity is an economic issue because only the rich can afford to pay bribes. Power corrupts in a hundred different ways: through abusing it to get money (John Murphy); or through wanting more power (Carol Bellamy); or through losing power (Ted Sorensen); or through needing to keep power (Ed Koch). And there is depicted here a permanent government of private institutions that is often more powerful than the elected representative government.

Yes, I have met some heroes and heroines over the last twenty years, but of diverse distinctions, origins, and qualities. With the luxury of hindsight, I can now recognize some characteristics they shared that compelled my admiration. Courage. A capacity for growth. Tenacity. A liberalism in politics, and perhaps a certain conservatism in life-style that I suspect provided the stability and discipline necessary for heroic conduct. But they also seem different in as many ways as they seem alike.

Muhammad Ali, the Muslim manchild free spirit and fighter of genius; Bill Moyers, the Baptist divinity student from small-town Texas who quoted Emily Dickinson and is now dazzling in his third career; Marcy Benstock, the relentless, antimaterialistic, Naderite woman warrior against the highway lobby; Robert Kennedy, born into privilege and celebrity, who became the tribune of the dispossessed; and Bob Moses, a black intellectual from Harlem who became a civil rights legend in Mississippi during the 1960s.

Perhaps the closest thing to a common denominator in some (but not all) of these articles is anger. When the particular has made me angry, I have not concealed that emotion from the reader. I find that anger—a sense of outrage—can be liberating for the creative process—if it is disciplined. Anger improves lucidity, persistence, audacity, and memory.

Anger can be therapeutic for both the writer and the reader. Compassion without the element of anger can become merely sentiment, or pity. And knowledge without anger can stagnate into mere cynicism and apathy.

At sporadic moments, however, I have secretly envied the more meditative and mellow prose of journalists like Murray Kempton, Richard Rovere, and Joseph Lash. But a writer's disposition and writing style are involuntary. Also, envy and self-image are complicated. One of the legendary, malice-free moralists is

Richard Strout, who, until April of 1983, published as "TRB" in the *New Republic*. Occasionally I wished I could acquire TRB's reasonable tone. But when Richard Strout, at age eighty-five, delivered a farewell address at the National Press Club in Washington, he counseled anger.

"I have advice for fellow journalists," Strout said. "I hope they will retain their curiosity, and at their heart a touch of anger. When the adrenaline runs low, when the little flare of anger flickers out, I think it is time for a reporter to think about going into some more remunerative form of work."

Permit me a few reflections on the craft of journalism.

I think that the basic problem with my profession is that it is divided into two segregated schools. There are reporters who are not encouraged to think, or to use their minds independently. And there are columnists, who have opinions, but do little original reporting or research. Because of this artificial division of labor, the subsurface reality of events—and the meaning of events—is often unknown to the people. Neither the pundit nor the clerk of facts supplies knowledge.

Reporters tend to get reduced to stenographers by the powerful. The formulas and conventions of newspapers require reporters to write down and quote whatever presidents, important politicians, and corporation executives say—even if it is not true, even if it has all been said before. Because of this mechanistic definition of news, Joe McCarthy became a national menace to liberty during the 1950s. Newspapers and television reported his reckless assertions simply because a senator was saying them, without taking the time to investigate the accuracy of the claims.

On the other hand, columnists, under the endless pressure of deadlines to produce three or four products every week, have little time to do any fresh reporting or thinking. They become unwitting self-parodists: Evans and Novak discover the last remnant of McGovernism again; Joe Kraft explains the last ten years in the Middle East after a private hour with the King of Jordan; Jack Anderson—the McDonald's of muckraking—hypes a trivial study into the next Watergate.

But there have always been reporters—and writers of books —who have broken barriers, evolved new styles, and integrated

these two segregated schools. There have always been nonconform-
ists who tried to synthesize facts with meaning, detail with history, statistics with passion, and new information with understanding. This is what Tom Paine and John Milton did in their
great essays. Jacob Riis and Lincoln Steffens mastered this craft
more than seventy-five years ago. This is what I. F. Stone, Murray
Kempton, and Seymour Hersh do so brilliantly. It is a synthesis
that Robert Caro, Rachel Carson, and Ralph Nader have accomplished in astonishing books.

Almost all of the pieces in this book were conceived in the
specific and begin with the empirical. A document was received
in the mail. A public event occurred. An article or book was read
that touched a nerve. An injured party appeared on my doorstep.

That is the way I work. I tend to be skeptical of theory,
abstraction, generalization, and ideology. I can only go from the
particular to the general, never the reverse. I become interested
in a specific fact, or circumstance, or institution, and then saturate
myself in the details. I have a capacity for obsession. Some of the
longer investigative articles in this collection (John Murphy and
the gang of landlord-arsonists) took more than six months to
research and write. I devoted almost two years to repeated follow-
ups about Bernard Bergman, the nursing home monster, until he
was indicted, convicted, and went to prison.

I try to apply the fact-collecting methods of investigative
reporting to essays of opinion about anti-Semitism and Mayor
Koch. And I try to apply thinking about causes and effects to
reporting the mistreatment of the powerless elderly in nursing
homes, and the death of a fighter in the ring.

These attempts don't always work, and sometimes the methods are fallible. But I think they offer the best hope of understanding what's really happening in the world, of at least trying to
comprehend some meaning that is deeper than the superficial
sum of press releases, official sources, ghost-written speeches, and
carefully scripted public ceremonies. If I know anything, it is that
the whole truth of history is never the way any government
presents it the first day.

Journalists ought to be willing to take the intellectual risks of
venturing beyond the safe commercial and reportorial formulas—
when the circumstances warrant it. The First Amendment was

not written in order to protect money-making contests, gossip columns, and stories that end with a recipe. It was written into the Constitution on the supposition that newspapers would play an important salutary role as the watchdog of government.

Investigative reporting is not glamorous. It is mostly boring, lonely, and frustrating. I have no secretary, no assistant, and no researcher. The daily routine of my work consists of: politicians not returning my phone calls; nights spent reassuring and calming useful sources who tend to be more given to conspiracy theories than I am; clipping and filing; studying financial documents that make me regret that I did not attend Harvard Business School for a year; typing Freedom of Information requests to bureaucrats; making index cards from old lists of campaign contributors; answering phone calls from disgruntled litigants and certified lunatics; and dealing with libel suits filed for purposes of harassment or intimidation (I've never lost one).

So at least, even in retrospect, I cannot honestly say there is one single system of thought unifying these pieces, written over a twenty-year period for the *Village Voice*. I think I've grown wiser and become a more careful writer over these seasons, and more respectful of ambiguity and of history. And come closer to inner peace. But I also hope I have been stubborn about retaining the values I acquired during the 1960s, when Robert Kennedy, Martin Luther King, and Bob Moses of SNCC were my tutors-by-example. If there is anything here approaching thematic unity, it is that the people, experiences, and facts contained here comprise my education in life.

1

The Rabbi Exposed and Anti-Semitism

Between December of 1974 and September of 1976, I wrote fifteen articles about corruption in the nursing home industry. Many of these articles focused on an orthodox rabbi named Bernard Bergman, who owned a cartel of homes, and dominated the association of nursing home operators.

I stumbled into this series through the back door. I was originally interested in an insurance brokerage company, owned by two Brooklyn clubhouse politicians, named Grand Brokerage. When I got a client list from the insurance company, I noticed the nursing homes. Then I became intrigued when I discovered the homes were operated by a politically influential religious leader. More document reading showed the rabbi's homes had hundreds of violations of the health code, and serious complaints from the relatives of patients. At that point, the subject of my story shifted from the insurance company to the nursing homes.

After I wrote the first two articles, employees of the homes, children of patients in the homes, and nurses and nurses' aides in hospitals near the homes started to call me with horror stories of patient neglect and financial chicanery.

A nurse at Brooklyn Jewish Hospital told me that when one of Bergman's patients was close to death, the nursing home would quickly transfer the comatose person to her hospital, so the nursing home would have a statistically low mortality rate. This nurse told me the hospital staff used the phrase "Bergman syndrome" as shorthand to describe a patient with infected bedsores, malnutrition, and dehydration.

In the end, Bernard Bergman pleaded guilty to stealing $2.5 million from Medicaid and trying to bribe a public official. He served separate federal and state prison sentences. But for many confusing months he roared his innocence; defiantly accused me and other reporters of McCarthyism during testimony before a Senate committee; and claimed in a series of interviews that he was a victim of anti-Semitism.

The controversy contributed to my self-awareness, although I did not enjoy it while it was going on, since Bergman was clever at putting me on the defensive, and the facts into question. I got letters and phone calls saying I was hurting the Jews; damaging Israel during the Arab oil embargo; and writing these miserable slanders because I was a typical self-hating Jew.

None of this criticism deterred me from continuing the investigation into Bergman, but it did cause me to brood and question my own motives. I thought I had relatively healthy and secure feelings of ethnic pride, derived from my childhood and strengthened by my close relationship for several years to a family that had survived the Holocaust. But the claims of "Jewish self-hatred" still hurt.

In the midst of the Bergman debate—and partly because of it—I visited Israel in March of 1975. The brief journey had no instant, dramatic effects, but it did gradually deepen my feelings of Jewish identity, and motivate me to study Israeli politics much more closely. In fact, in July of 1982 I signed one of the first advertisements protesting Israel's invasion of Lebanon—three months before the massacre at the two refugee camps. It was the same statement signed by Saul Bellow, Rabbi Balfour Brickner, Irving Howe, Michael Walzer, and others with whom I share a generally liberal domestic outlook coupled with a commitment to Israel's existence.

The nursing home series was a breakthrough for me; it taught me lessons I prize. One was the imperative of the repeated follow-up article. Another was the value of cooperation with other reporters I respect, in order to get the story out. I wrote about the abuse of the elderly not to document it, but to stop it. So I collaborated closely with John Hess of *The New York Times*, and Steve Bauman of WNEW-TV. This sort of camaraderie and coordination is considered unorthodox conduct by most media executives. But our mutual objective was not institutional glory or individual prizes; it was exposure and reform. So we shared information and traded documents in what for months was a detective story whose end we did not know. Without Hess and Bauman, the public would never have become so aroused, and so aware.

The feisty and gifted Hess took the greatest risk, because his bosses were blindly hostile to the idea of muckraker solidarity from below, and some of Hess's most important stories had already been mangled, delayed, and buried in the back of the paper by editors. And without Bauman, the complete facts would have never reached the broader audience of television.

Nailing Bergman took two years. Cleaning up the nursing home industry will take forever. Our success was only partial at best, and I'm confident I will write about nursing homes again.

"Anti-Semitism and the Crime of Silence" was written for many reasons, some of which, at least in my unconscious, probably go back to my thoughts and feelings while working on the nursing home series five years earlier.

The immediate inspiration was reading Jacobo Timerman's book, *Prisoner Without a Name, Cell Without a Number*. It affected me the way *Darkness at Noon* and *1984* had affected me.

And the book forced me to reflect on the fact that the *Voice* had failed to place a high priority upon the rights of Jews as an injured minority with quite the same fervor that it had vigilantly defended the rights of other disrespected minorities—blacks, gays, artists, union insurgents, the elderly. Partly I wrote the piece to clean my own house.

A second motive for writing the essay was my desire to express myself on the need for a single standard for human rights in the world.

A single democratic standard for human rights should be a most appealing intellectual concept. But I saw it regularly violated by the Podhoretz-Kirkpatrick Right, and by the Kunstler-Baraka Left. People like Podhoretz would only object to injustices in communist countries like Russia and Cuba, while people like Kunstler would only object to deprivations of liberty in right-wing countries like South Africa and Argentina. I felt it was important

to stick up for the single universal ideal of freedom, regardless of
what label a tyrant placed on his system of misrule.

In the end, the most important fact about Bernard Bergman
was not that he was a rabbi. It was that he was predator, an
economic ghoul. His patients were the victims. Just as Timerman
was a victim, and the Jews in the Soviet Union are victims. That
is the paradox of these two pieces—the Jew as victim, and the Jew
as victimizer. The consistent thread is anger at the overdog, and
identification with the casualty—regardless of religion.

REFLECTIONS ON HUNTING BERGMAN

I confess to a measure of satisfaction from the state and federal
criminal indictments of Bernard Bergman this week. I had spent
four months writing a series of nine articles about him. I had
absorbed so many interviews and documents that I dreamed
about Bergman and his nursing homes. Bergman became my
obsession, my personal Moby Dick hovering on the horizon.

I had become uncomfortably embattled in the course of writing the Bergman story. My credibility had been challenged by
Bergman in his appearance before a committee of the United
States Senate. I received letters accusing me of anti-Semitism and
Jewish self-hatred. To be a protagonist in such a confrontation,
without certainty of vindication, can cause anxiety, frustration,
and self-doubt. What follows are some memories and reflections
of my participation in the hunt for this white whale of free
enterprise.

The first thing that made me aware of Bernard Bergman was
reading Mary Adelaide Mendelson's seminal book on the nursing

home industry, *Tender Loving Greed.* Then I received a tip that Assemblyman Stanley Steingut was Bergman's insurance broker, and Steingut's counsel, Daniel Chill, was one of Bergman's lawyers. Such an exacta of connivers alerted my instincts for a possible scandal.

John Hess of *The New York Times* had already written several fine pieces on nursing homes, so I called him and invited him to dinner at my home. Hess, a rebel at the Times, generously urged me to jump into the story.

"Those bastards at the *Times* are cutting my stories and burying them," he said. "They tell me nursing homes is a 'noncompetitive story,' which means the editors think no one is interested. They've held up my last piece for a week now. But, believe me, Bergman is the worst. And he's going to get away with everything, unless someone like you picks up the story."

The specific evidence of Bergman's payroll padding and concealed subsubcase ownership was not that hard to find. It was all there, in the archives of government itself: at the Stein Commission, in the city and state health departments, in HEW's regional office. And at the office of the state welfare inspector general, where a compulsive assistant named Bill Cabin worked till midnight and on weekends to assemble documents like concealed checks and incorporation papers, and accounting ledgers, while his boss, William Meyers, tried to discourage the inquiry at this incipient stage.

Meyers, a crony of nursing home owner and power broker Charles Sigety, finally ordered Cabin to take a vacation, changed the lock on his office, and gave him no work to do when he returned.

If there is an unknown soldier in the Bergman fall, it is young Cabin, who risked his job last November for no reward.

I could sense quickly that it was going to be a big political story. I knew this because Dan Chill, Stanley Steingut's legislative counsel, would not talk to me. I called him every day for a week and left messages in his law office in Brooklyn. Then I asked a mutual friend to find out why Chill was ducking me. The mutual friend told me Chill was "scared" and would not see me under any circumstances. I knew then Chill had something to hide, and I had something to find. This was last November.

I have a theory about muckraking. The follow-up is decisive.
Any bureaucracy, any institution, any industry can survive one or
two embarrassing articles. It is only repeated exposure, with fact
piled upon fact, that makes a difference. My goal is usually to try
to remedy some policy or omission of government. And this can
best be attempted with the bludgeons of endurance, memory, and
detail.

As soon as I published my first two pieces on Bergman, I
began to receive phone calls from citizens who had personal
experiences with Bergman's nursing homes. Nurses who worked
inside his homes called. People whose parents died in Bergman
homes called. A resident of the Hotel Brewster, who had two
shopping bags filled with documents on Bergman's real estate
holdings, delivered them to my home one Sunday night. Two
neighbors, who lived in Bergman's apartment building on River-
side Drive, called to say that he even mistreated the doormen and
handymen of his own building.

I met with a couple of Hasidic Jews in Brooklyn, who told me
(after I prayed with them) that Bergman's parents had been
convicted of smuggling heroin concealed in Hebrew prayer books.
A mysterious woman, very frightened, who claimed to have
known Bergman for twenty-five years, began to call me at home
and tell me stories of Bergman's life.

"Bergman's only God is money," she said, more than once.

She also said, "You're wasting your time. He's too powerful.
You will never catch Bergman. He only deals with cash. You can
never prove anything."

It felt as if my first articles had rubbed a raw, dormant nerve
in the city. I had written about judges and bankers and landlords,
but I had never gotten such a voluntary, spontaneous outpouring
of sources. It almost seemed that every life Bergman touched, he
diminished or exploited.

Only one person had a kind word to say about Bergman. This
person, an acquaintance whom I will call G, arranged dinner with
me one night early in my research. He pleaded with me not to
write about Bergman at all. He argued it would be "dangerous to
Jews" and "damaging to Jews in general," if I wrote about Bergman (an orthodox rabbi) at a historic moment when Israel's existence was in jeopardy. And at a time when there seemed to be
an upsurge of anti-Semitism around the world.

To gain sympathy, Bergman himself had used the baseless allegation that he was a victim of anti-Semitism. Both Sam Hausman and Dan Chill testified before the Moreland Act Commission that Bergman had complained to them of anti-Jewish prejudice by the state health department. This claim was a nadir of chutzpah, since Bergman received every privilege and protection government could bestow, despite the fact he cheated on Medicaid, neglected patients, and had a generally rotten reputation.

G's argument—that by writing the truth about Bergman, I might be harming all Jews—was offensive to me. I had once been close to a woman who was a survivor of Auschwitz, and I understood the consequences of real anti-Semitism quite well. I was enough in touch with my own feelings of pride in being Jewish to feel secure about my motives in writing about Bergman.

A few weeks later, Bergman's henchmen—especially Stanley Steingut and Stanley Lowell—began spreading rumors that John Hess was anti-Semitic. It made me feel better that Andrew Stein and I were Jewish; naively, I thought this would limit religious polarization and paranoia.

Then I got what appeared to be an organized series of letters accusing me of "Jewish self-hatred." Despite my confidence in my own motives, such an allegation against the unconscious is impossible for anyone to refute, and after a while I did begin to feel misunderstood and defensive.

But then a friend reminded me that the Italians thought I was anti-Italian when I wrote about Judge Rinaldi, the Puerto Ricans claimed I was anti-Hispanic when I wrote about Joe Erazo, and the *Amsterdam News* called me a racist when I listed a black judge as one of the ten worst.

"Maybe the Greek Orthodox will give you a brotherhood award. You haven't attacked one of them yet," my friend said.

Bergman exploited his religious role in more ways than one. Not only did he try to intimidate his critics by charging them with anti-Semitism, but he—and people like Sam Hausman, Stanley Lowell, and Dan Chill—used the world of Jewish and Israeli philanthropy as a temple for their money making.

Bergman contributed to charitable groups to acquire social respectability and meet people with influence. Politicians let Bergman use them because they wanted access to Bergman's world—campaign contributions, legitimacy with an ethnic group that voted as a bloc, and endorsements from rabbis.

It was a symbiotic back scratching. Bergman made political connections. Sam Hausman's nephew was going to become a licensee of a nursing home. Dan Chill got $12,000 in legal fees and was to get a 14 percent ownership interest in one home. Stanley Lowell made enough money for a lifetime. Bergman arranged for Hausman's friend Nelson Rockefeller to be the guest of honor at the annual dinner of the Religious Zionists of America; Hausman got Bergman two private meetings with Governor Malcolm Wilson.

And no one felt any guilt because it was all done in an atmosphere of virtue—doing good for Israel, or for Soviet Jews. I suspect that Stanley Lowell actually felt proud when he told people that John Hess was anti-Semitic.

But the Bergman crowd did not invent this form of cynicism. A few years ago, Meyer Lansky accused mob muckraker Hank Messick of anti-Semitism and then used some of his Las Vegas skim to make a contribution to Brandeis University.

I have been asked several times why I think the investigative reporting we did about nursing homes was relatively successful in terms of governmental response and results.

A major factor, I think, was the cooperation, the sharing of ideas and information, between Hess, Steve Bauman, and myself. We each kept certain of our sources secret, and we each approached the story from our individual perspectives. But the fact we were getting very complex information to the public, from three separate media, reinforced our impact.

On television, Bauman was able to show the lonely vulnerability of real victims. Bauman also put together a superb documentary special. I was able to emphasize the role of politicians like Stanley Steingut and Al Blumenthal in obtaining preferential treatment for Bergman in exchange for legal fees, campaign contributions, and insurance business. Hess was able to write almost every day, piling up the evidence with professionalism under deadline pressure.

Bergman could have outlasted any of us individually. His wealth and political connections had kept him immune from indictment since the 1950s. Only our coordinated efforts, plus

Andrew Stein's persistent exposures, created a climate where a newly elected governor felt compelled to act; Carey appointed Joe Hynes as special prosecutor for nursing homes on January 10.

Too often, if one paper breaks a story, rival papers will purposefully ignore it, or even make an effort to knock it down. For several months in 1972, the "responsible" and "objective" dinosaurs of *The New York Times* seemed to regard the impeachable crimes of Watergate as merely hallucinations by Bob Woodward and Carl Bernstein. When Seymour Hersh of the *Times* first revealed the CIA's "massive illegal domestic spying" last December, the *Washington Post* reciprocated the petty conduct.

As a professional canon, I think the public interest should come before ego rivalries that exist primarily inside the heads of editors and publishers.

On January 21, 1975, Bergman testified before the United States Senate, at a crowded hearing at 14 Vesey Street. Bergman gave a brilliant performance, denying everything, and convincing many neutral observers that he might be a victim of McCarthyism. I will quote part of Bergman's prepared statement of that day because of its eloquent plausability.

"Over the past few months I have been the target of a program of litigation and abuse from public officials, and especially by the media, which, I think, has no parallel in modern American history since the days of Joseph McCarthy. . . . All of these allegations—and the many that will follow in their wake—are false, are incorrect, are untrue.

"The entire history of this barrage of accusations distresses me for many reasons, beyond the great personal anguish and discomfort it has caused to me and my family. It has proved to me, and to those who know me, that the average citizen of the United States is powerless in the face of the big lie repeated often enough from sources that seem, at least superficially, respectable.

"That is, I think, a great danger to freedom in this country. I move to stress that these charges have smeared not just me and my family, but many individuals whom I have known, businesses I have dealt with, even attorneys I have retained. . . .

"I'm neither less nor more interested in profits than *The New York Times* or the *Village Voice* are interested in theirs. And I believe I run my business as lawfully as they run theirs. And, I am sure, with a little more consideration for the rights of the individual."

Bergman denied virtually everything we had written about him. For the next few days I was struck by passing moods of self-doubt. What if I was wrong? What if I had misunderstood all the Medicaid reimbursement forms and audits and title searches I had studied? Could there be two Bernard Bergmans who owned nursing homes, making Bergman justified in calling it "a case of mistaken identity"?

Self-doubt can be a valuable asset to an investigative reporter. It can prevent excesses and carelessness. It can help you appreciate ambiguity. But eventually I remembered it was misplaced in the case of Bergman.

Soon another variety of self-doubt surfaced. Were my stories violating Bergman's civil liberties? Was I contributing to prejudicial pretrial publicity that might deny Bergman the fair trial the Constitution guaranteed to every citizen? As a radical Democrat, I regard the Bill of Rights as one of the few sacred texts. So what was the point of my writing a tenth or eleventh exposé of Bergman? A special prosecutor, whom I knew and trusted, had finally been appointed. The matter was now in his legal jurisdiction. So I decided early in March to stop writing about Bergman, even though several people I respect thought it was a premature decision.

Somewhere in this city, there is a Bergman of day care leases, a Bergman of private methadone clinics, a Bergman of Medicaid clinics, a Bergman of real estate. I want to find and write about those people, too.

A lot of politicians and a lot of journalists like to make fun of Andrew Stein. They ridicule his wealth, his father, his hunger for publicity, his blind spot toward his benefactor, Nelson Rockefeller. I used to make some of these cruel jokes myself.

But having watched Stein closely over the past nine months, my opinion has changed. I think he has grown. Stein has liberated himself by becoming an outsider.

Stein decided politics should not be a wrestling charade of fake public posturing and private comraderie and business deals. Stein started to get emotional about the infected bedsores he saw, about all the Medicaid money he saw go into the bank accounts of nursing home owners and investors instead of into patient care. Stein took his personal feelings into public places. He blew the whistle on the legislative leaders of his own party. That's why the establishment ostracized him. He disrupted the polite game politicians play with outrage that wasn't counterfeit.

The indictment of Bernard Bergman is not the end of the journey. Bergman became a symbol. But the system still exists. Solomon Heilser and Frank Klein and others are still making millions of dollars from Medicaid rip-offs. It is a whole industry that needs purification. Bergman should not be a scapegoat for an entire economy of corruption.

The profit-making incentive still endures as a magnet for the greedy. Medicaid still reimburses nursing home owners for legal fees and public relations campaigns. The state legislature killed the ethics reform bill that would have prevented lawyer-legislators from representing clients before state agencies. And so far, none of the politicians who did favors for Bergman have been indicted.

The end of the journey will be dignity and better quality care for all senior citizens. The end of the journey will be a more respectful way of thinking about old age itself.

In my lifetime in this city, I have never encountered anyone as rotten as Bernard Bergman.

I have seen slumlords who gouged welfare tenants out of a few extra dollars of rent. I have seen muggers who hurt blind news-dealers, and then stole their seeing-eye dogs. I have seen judges who are corrupt and bigoted.

But Bernard Bergman, in a certain sense, is the worst. He is the worst because he is the most respectable. And he has gotten away with it all.

Bergman has money, power, and respect. His wealth is estimated at $100 million. His contributions to charities are legendary. His respect comes out of the hundreds of awards he has received, the hundreds of dinners where he sat on the dias. It comes, too, from the fact that he is an Orthodox rabbi, one of the world leaders of the Mizrachi movement.

But what kind of a Jew is Bergman?

He bills Medicaid for dead people. His feeble patients must lie in their own urine all night because there is no staff on duty. Bergman's goons tried to evict the elderly residents of the

Brewster Hotel, calling them "old pieces of shit" in Yiddish. Where in the Talmud is such conduct approved?

The symbol of Bergman's relationship to God is what happened in 1941, when Bergman's mother and father were convicted of smuggling eight kilos of heroin into the United States. The heroin was concealed in the bindings of Hebrew prayer books.

The fact is that the Bergmans of this world are one cause of anti-Semitism. Bergman is now trying to manipulate the image of God, the same way his parents used the Holy Book to hide the heroin.

August 11, 1975

THE CRIME OF ANTI-SEMITISM

Anti-Semitism is the socialism of fools.
—BEBEL

More than a year ago I began to keep a file on anti-Semitism. Each time a swastika was spray-painted on a synagogue, each time the U.S. Labor party blamed the heroin traffic or the murder of Jimmy Hoffa on a Jewish conspiracy, each time the government of Poland tried to stir up anti-Semitism to divide the workers of Solidarity, each time the Liberty Lobby claimed the Holocaust never happened, each time there was an act of terrorism directed against the Jews by the PLO or neo-Nazi groups, I clipped the article and filed it. A few times I made follow-up phone calls to pin down the details.

I am Jewish and I have a healthy amount of ethnic pride. I once half-jokingly told Stokley Carmichael that I felt no race guilt toward him, but that he should have class guilt toward me, since he went to the elite Bronx High School of Science, while I had attended predominantly black and dilapidated Boys High in Bed-Stuy.

I visited Israel in 1975, and was gradually affected by the experience, although I was never an admirer of the militaristic Begin government. I have had close friends who survived Nazi concentration camps, and Israel, for all its imperfections, has always seemed a necessary sanctuary from a future Holocaust. To me, modern Zionism is a defensive response to anti-Semitism. The Zionism-equals-racism slogan is one of the great lies of this century of great lies.

Over fifteen years, I have written only three or four articles that dealt with the crime of anti-Semitism. The subject has not been a recurring theme of mine, the way abuses by landlords, judges, politicians, nursing home operators, or union racketeers have been.

This abdication was one reason why I began to collect material early last year. Anti-Semitism should be among the concerns of any writer who claims to be a tribune of underdogs, of any writer who claims to be a critic of injustice.

The *Village Voice* has been my home for seventeen years. And it has become painful to me that my own house is not as concerned about anti-Semitism as I wish it were. The *Voice*, to its everlasting credit, has played a significant role in defending the rights of other groups that are discriminated against—blacks, women, gays, union dissidents, artists. The *Voice* has been a vigilant watchdog on abortion, civil liberties, and militarism. But the rights of Jews have been a secondary concern. Jewish nationalism has been treated differently from every other nationalism.

Partly I blame myself for this, because I did not write enough about it. Colleagues like Paul Cowan and Ellen Willis have published some superb articles. But they are not in this paper frequently enough to offset the impression that the much more prolific Alexander Cockburn gives to most readers.

It is somewhat difficult for me to write about Alex because he is a friend who occupies the adjacent office, someone with whom I agree on most issues. But Alex has one gigantic blind spot. Or, more precisely, three blind spots that converge. And Alex's blind spot gives people the impression that this house is deaf to the problems of Jews.

Alex has a dual standard of human rights that makes it almost impossible for him to criticize communist human-rights violators, whether they are in Vietnam or in the Soviet Union, where those persecuted include Jews. Alex is anti-West, which leads him to despise America's ally, Israel, although he has never been to Israel. And Alex supports the PLO, which is committed to "the liquidation of the Zionist entity, politically, militarily, culturally, and ideologically."

Since Alex writes much more frequently than any other *Voice* writer, these elements combine to create an image of the *Voice* as insensitive to Jewish concerns. I do not believe Alex is prejudiced. But he is a political accountant who keeps two sets of books.

Over the last seven years, Alex has written well over a hundred articles and shorter items condemning Israel and accurately pointing out abuses of the rights of Palestinians. But during the same period of time, Alex has written virtually no words of protest about Anatoly Shcharansky, or Ida Nudel, or Alexander Ginzberg, or other casualties of Russia's savage anti-Semitism. No polemics of censure for the PLO's murder of school children at Ma'alot, or pregnant women at Kiryat Shmona. No essays about the unequal status of women in Arab nations, no columns on the 1981 Amnesty International report on the sexual torture of political prisoners by Iraq.

In 1978, Alex followed the counsel of Noam Chomsky rather than I. F. Stone, condemning the Camp David peace accords and Anwar Sadat for selling out the PLO. And last month Alex endorsed the absurd, authoritarian attempt by Soviet, Arab, and third-world nations in UNESCO to "license" journalists and require us to wear "identity cards," which could be revoked by the state if any inconvenient facts are reported. A press critic who justifies censorship is the ultimate fox in the chicken coop.

I will always defend Alex's right to publish his views in the *Voice*. But I doubt that they represent the thinking of most of the people who work here.

Part of what has moved me, at last, to declare my interest is that I now see and smell and hear a surge in anti-Semitism both in this country and around the world. I see it among teenage vandals and crank callers to cable TV shows seeking scapegoats for economic hard times. I see it much more dangerously among right-wing organizations like the Liberty Lobby, the U.S. Labor party, and in a more subtle form, in the Moral Majority and the fundamentalist, evangelical New Right.

The annual study released by the Anti-Defamation League showed a sharp rise in anti-Semitic assaults, arsons, and vandalism in 1980. The study showed 377 such incidents reported last year, compared with 129 in 1979 and 49 in 1978. In part this seems the result of a better reporting system by ADL, but it also seems to reflect a climate in which anti-Semites feel freer to express their prejudice. In the last two years, the bigoted rantings of "celebrities" like Billy Carter and Spiro Agnew have gotten attention on the TV talk-show circuit, and I suspect this helps confer legitimacy upon darker impulses.

The Reverend Dan Fore, the chairman of the Moral Majority in New York State, was quoted by Joyce Purnick in the February 5, 1981 *New York Times* as saying: "Jews have a God-given ability to make money, almost a supernatural ability to make money. . . . They control the media, they control this city."

Last October my friend Pete Hamill returned from a month traveling in the fundamentalist South, and told me he found a disturbing amount of anti-Jewish feeling. Some of the people he met blamed "the Jews" for America's failure in Vietnam, and regarded them as alien intruders in Christian America.

In a speech last August in Dallas that was shown several times on network television, Bailey Smith, the president of the thirteen-million-member Southern Baptist Convention, said: "God Almighty does not hear the prayer of the Jew, for how in the world can God hear the prayer of a man who says Jesus Christ is not the true Messiah?"

In February of this year, the Valentine's Day issue of the Lynbrook, Long Island, High School newspaper published an anti-Semitic ad that had been approved by school administrators.

"To the princess," the ad said. "It's been a GAS knowing Yews. Meet us in the showers." The ad included a Star of David.

Newsday reporter Kathleen Kerr interviewed the mother of one of the students who placed the ad. The mother said: "If those girls keep flaunting their wealth, what can you expect?"

In France, since early 1979, there has been a wave of anti-

Semitic violence. Dozens of young people were injured in the bombing of a kosher restaurant. A bomb was placed under the car of Nazi hunter Serge Klarsfeld. Bombs were placed outside the Olympic Cinema during Jewish Culture Week. And Pierre Goldman, the radical author of *Obscure Memories of a Polish Jew Born in France,* was assassinated by the extreme right on his way to visit his wife in the maternity ward.

In West Germany, three prominent Jewish civic leaders have been assassinated in the last six months. An article published last month in *Der Spiegel* established funding, weapons, and training connections between neo-Nazi terrorists in Germany and the PLO. European terrorists of the right and left agree on their hatred of Jews and Israel, just as both Hitler and Stalin hated Jews.

I see an unexpected tolerance of anti-Semitism by the Reagan administration, an administration elected with a large share of Jewish votes yet without a single Jew in its cabinet. It is planning to supply weapons and money to the torturers who run Argentina, and is anxious to supply AWACs to Saudi Arabia, whose petroleum profits subsidize PLO terrorism.

And just as some on the left have a double standard about democracy, some conservatives, particularly Jewish conservatives, are surprisingly silent, as Jews suffer a limited holocaust in Argentina. *Commentary* editor Norman Podhoretz, for example, has conspicuously abstained from any criticism of Reagan's alliance with the generals who rule Argentina with state terrorism. Since the military seized power in 1976, an estimated 20,000 Argentine citizens are "missing"—defense lawyers of political prisoners, professors, psychologists, journalists, and Jews.

Jacobo Timerman's torturers kept asking him: "Are you a Jew?" "Are you a Zionist?"

Podhoretz failed to join those who insisted that an end to official anti-Semitism in Argentina be a *precondition* to America's supplying arms to that government. Podhoretz supported the nomination of Ernest Lefever, while Lefever was being opposed by the American Jewish Congress, the Committee for Soviet Jewry, the Helsinki Watch Committee, and the Union of American Hebrew Congregations.

Norman Podhoretz, America's tough Jewish cop, suddenly

seems willing to tolerate the torture of Jews, as long as the torturers say they are anti-Soviet.

I write this article from the first principle of a single standard
of democratic humanism. All bigotry, all persecution, is equally
abhorrent, whether it is practiced against Catholics in Northern
Ireland, blacks in New York City, Palestinians on the West Bank
of the River Jordan, or Jews in the Soviet Union.

We cannot create two classes of victim in the world based on
abstract ideological prejudices. The rights of the Kurds are as
important as the rights of the American Indians. The rights of the
Afghans are as important as the rights of the Salvadorans. The
rights of women in Saudi Arabia are as important as the rights of
gays in Cuba.

Freedom and equality are universal imperatives. Archbishop
Romero of El Salvador, Steven Biko of South Africa, Jacobo
Timerman of Argentina, Lech Walesa of Poland, Elie Wiesel of
Buchenwald, Andrei Sakharov of the Soviet Union, and Martin
Luther King, they are all my brothers.

Jacobo Timerman's book *Prisoner Without a Name, Cell
Without a Number* is only 164 pages long. But it is one of the
most emotionally devastating books I have ever read. It ranks with
the works of Orwell, Solzhenitsyn, Koestler, Kafka, and Hannah
Arendt as an expedition into the totalitarian mind.

The essential mentality of Argentina's generals was captured
by Timerman's quotation from one theoretician of the regime.

"Argentina has three main enemies. Karl Marx because he
tried to destroy the Christian concept of society; Sigmund Freud
because he tried to destroy the Christian concept of family; and
Albert Einstein because he tried to destroy the Christian concept
of time and space."

The three Jewish geniuses of the modern world are all enemies
of the state in Argentina.

Jews are not the only people kidnapped, tortured, and murdered by the state in Argentina. Most of the 20,000 "missing"
people are not Jewish. But anti-Semitism is central to the sadis-
tic/paranoid/gangster mentality of Argentina's junta. The Jew is
their scapegoat. Being Jewish, Timerman writes, "is a category of
guilt."

Even before he was arrested, Timerman was told by a naval

officer of the regime: "Hitler lost the war. We will win." Timerman saw swastikas in the interrogation rooms. In the secret prisons, he writes, "Jewish girls were violated twice as often as other girls." The torturers chanted "Jew, Jew, Jew" and "clipped prick, clipped prick" as they sent the electric shocks into Timerman's testicles.

Timerman writes: "At times I felt like those Jews who wound up being convinced by the Nazis that they were objects of hatred because they were intrinsically hateful objects." But, of course, his spirit was too great to surrender to either self-hatred or to the bestiality of his abductors.

Timerman was in a clandestine jail for a total of thirty months without a trial. Finally, as a result of pressure from the international human rights movement—and especially from the Carter administration's Patricia Derian, who Lefever was supposed to replace—Timerman was released from prison in September of 1979. His newspaper was confiscated, his citizenship revoked, and he was deported to Israel, where he composed his book of witness.

Jacobo Timerman, back from the dead, is now the most dangerous man in the world to human-rights hypocrites like Secretary of State Alexander Haig, Jeane Kirkpatrick, Undersecretary of State James Buckley, and the rejected Lefever. And to Reaganite Jewish intellectuals like Podhoretz and Irving Kristol. Timerman's existence is a broken finger pointing at their appeasement of anti-Semitism.

Timerman is an old-fashioned Labor Zionist, a Jew, an anticommunist liberal who supported Allende and criticized Argentina's left-wing terrorists, a reflective and humane intellectual, a brave man, an eloquent witness with perfect memory. He is our Solzhenitsyn.

When Secretary of State Haig was asked by Congressman Gerry Studds of Massachusetts what values America shared with Argentina's generals other than anticommunism, Haig replied: "A belief in God."

But as Anthony Lewis rebutted for all of us in the *Times:* "Could he have meant the God of Torquemeda? Of the Cossacks who terrorized Jews? Of Julius Streicher?"

In 1979, Jeane Kirkpatrick published her notorious essay in *Commentary.* That article directly asserted the right-wing argument in favor of a conscious double standard on human rights. It claimed that Communist tyrannies are "totalitarian," and that right-wing, pro-American tyrannies are "authoritarian," and therefore more deserving of military aid and "quiet diplomacy."

Kirkpatrick claimed that "traditional autocrats" observe "traditional taboos" and respect "habitual patterns of family and personal relations."

But Timerman, the witness with memory, writes:

"Of all the dramatic situations I witnessed in clandestine prisons, nothing can compare to those family groups who were tortured often together, sometimes separately, but in view of one another. . . .

"The entire affective world, constructed over the years, with utmost difficulty, collapses with a kick in the father's genitals . . . or the sexual violation of a daughter. Suddenly, an entire culture based on familial love, devotion, and the capacity for mutual sacrifice collapses."

Timerman is such an extraordinary witness that a desperate, ugly campaign to injure his credibility has recently been launched by architects of Reagan's human rights policy.

(Admittedly, the emotional Timerman has said one or two things in spontaneous interviews that prosecutorial critics might say are exaggerations. But they are nothing compared to the many bizarre comments of Solzhenitsyn that are clearly antidemocratic and repressive. But these are ignored by those masters of the double standard who only wish to discredit Timerman.)

Undersecretary of State James Buckley (our former senator) assured the Congress of the United States on May 8 that the government of Argentina was not guilty of any anti-Semitic acts, a lie so preposterous that even William F. Buckley had to dispute it in a column in the *Daily News* of May 21. This was before Buckley got the party line straight and wrote another column on May 31 that questioned Timerman's sanity.

But in his May 21 column, William Buckley concluded that Argentina was, in fact, anti-Semitic, that "Brother James was wrong in his emphasis"; and observed: "What is distinctive to the Nazis is the association of torture with race: and this was Timerman's experience in Argentina."

Almost half of Buckley's May 31 column was taken up with

quotes from the legendary Nazi hunter Simon Wiesenthal attributed to a newspaper in Uruguay. Buckley quoted Wiesenthal as saying Timerman exaggerated about anti-Semitism; that Timerman was originally arrested because he favored terrorism; that Timerman had "leftist" views; and that Timerman should "stick to the truth."

To be attacked by Simon Wiesenthal must have felt like a new kind of psychological torture to Timerman. But it now turns out the quotes used by Buckley were a hoax. *Wiesenthal never said such things.* Buckley was so anxious to get them into print that he never attempted to verify their authenticity.

It further turns out that Buckley got the fabricated quotes from an aide to Jeane Kirkpatrick named Carl Gershman. Gershman is a frequent contributor to *Commentary.*

When a *New York Times* reporter informed Gershman that Wiesenthal had repudiated almost all the quotes slipped to Buckley, Gershman replied: "It's up to the journalist if he wants to check it out."

Podhoretz has attacked Timerman at meetings with Jewish leaders, and he told the *Times:* "Most of the Jews in Argentina, and most informed observers, don't agree with him."

But Rabbi Morton Rosenthal published an article called "Argentine Anti-Semitism, Again" in the January 1981 *Bulletin* of the Anti-Defamation League that reported an "ominous resurgence of overt anti-Semitism in Argentina." The ADL *Bulletin's* article also said: "Objective analysis of the record during the past four years shows that the government has failed to prevent anti-Semitism when it could readily have done so, or to punish those responsible for it."

I guess Podhoretz no longer accepts the ADL as an informed observer of bigotry in the world.

The most shameful smear of Timerman has come from Irving Kristol in a column in the May 29 *Wall Street Journal.* Kristol claimed that Timerman's defenders have ignored communist violations of human rights—a slur on Amnesty International, Anthony Lewis, and Timerman's publisher Bob Bernstein, the president of the Helsinki Watch Committee.

Kristol also tried to smear Timerman through guilt by association, twice removed. Kristol linked Timerman to the missing bank swindler, David Graiver, an investor in his newspaper, and then linked Graiver to left-wing terrorists who, Kristol insinuated, Timerman had allegiance to. The ADL's Rabbi Rosenthal has described the Kristol article as "a piece of character assassination."

Kristol's article concluded: "In effect, the Argentina Jewish community, along with several of the major American Jewish organizations, in keeping their distance from Mr. Timerman and his left-wing associates, are implicitly vindicating the Reagan administration's prudent policy on human rights. The military regime in Argentina, for all its ugly aspects, is authoritarian, not totalitarian."

This authoritarian/totalitarian dichotomy is a theological hallucination that has no relation to the real world. If there is any possible authoritarian/totalitarian distinction to be made, then the state's employment of systematic torture might be a logical place to draw the line. So might the freedom to organize an independent reform movement like Solidarity.

Argentina is a totalitarian regime. I would even describe it, with considered exactness, as a Nazi government. And so did several reviewers of Timerman's book, including Eliot Fremont-Smith in the *Voice*, John Leonard in the *Times*, Robert Cox in the *Washington Post's Book World*, and William Buckley in his May 21 column.

A single standard on human rights is not only in the best interests of the United States, it is also in the long-run interest of Israel.

The argument that Argentina is "just" authoritarian means that Saudi Arabia and Syria are also "just" authoritarian, and therefore politically acceptable. And eventually that logic robs Israel of any moral superiority even though it is one democracy surrounded by twenty Arab dictatorships. It shrinks Israel to being a strategic asset of the West, and nothing more.

The single standard is also in the interests of Soviet Jews, scientists, and dissidents imprisoned in labor camps, as several witnesses against the Lefever nomination pointed out. A politicized, propagandistic human rights policy that only attacked Soviet abuses would have no credibility and no effectiveness. This point was emphasized to me by several leading activists in the movement for Soviet Jewry, who care about results.

I would not want to be a Jew in a Soviet labor camp and hear my jailer tell me: "You see, the United States doesn't care about human rights in South Africa, or Argentina, or Guatemala. The United States just wants to use you to attack the Russian government. There is no principle at stake here. You're just a poor, stupid prop in the new cold war. The United States doesn't really care about individual liberty. They're just exploiting your suffering as a tactic."

I have only met Norman Podhoretz once. It was in 1969, during the New York City's school strike, at a meeting at the home of *Partisan Review* editor William Phillips. I remember the encounter vividly because Podhoretz and I had a shouting debate. Without knowing or asking what I actually thought, Podhoretz took me for an avatar of the New Left, and accused me of being "a typical self-hating Jew" who wanted to "shove the Jewish people back into the gas ovens." He also claimed that I was an enemy of Israel.

At the time I thought Podhoretz was obnoxious, but I was at least able to understand his extremist passion to protect Jewish interests. But now, after Haig, after Kirkpatrick, after Timerman, I believe that Podhoretz *uses Jewish interests* to promote his extreme ideological bias.

In 1969, Podhoretz had a strong public reaction to a few anti-Semitic leaflets distributed by a powerless, fringe faction of blacks during the school strike. He was also infuriated by an anti-Semitic poem written by a twelve-year-old girl. Today in Argentina, *the government* has kidnapped and tortured more than 1200 Jews; there are blatantly anti-Semitic programs on the state-owned television stations; there are publicly displayed photos of Hitler and swastikas on the walls of the torture cells. Yet Podhoretz indicates there is nothing for Jews to get alarmed about.

If I had the opportunity to renew my quarrel with Podhoretz today, I would quote to him what Timerman said to the Israeli leader Yigal Allon: "I had not been humiliated by torture, or by the electric shocks on my genitals, but had been profoundly humiliated by the silent complicity of Jewish leaders."

When I was beginning my political education in the early 1960s, there was an almost automatic identification between Jews and the left. I associated anti-Semitism almost exclusively with the political right; with the Spanish Inquisition; with the pogroms in Europe during the 1840s and again during the 1880s; with the prosecutors of Dreyfus; with Hitler's crematoria; with Franco's Spain and the Vichy government of France; with the Ku Klux Klan, Father Coughlin, and Joe McCarthy.

The intellectuals of the democratic left who influenced me twenty years ago were all vigilant against anti-Semitism, and they all cared about the survival of Israel. I am thinking of Irving Howe, Mike Harrington, Murray Kempton, Hannah Arendt, Dwight Macdonald, I. F. Stone, and Norman Mailer.

But, gradually, over the last ten or fifteen years, a segment of the American left has grown less and less sensitive to anti-Semitism. And more indifferent about the existence of Israel.

There are a multitude of reasons for this shift, and I can only guess at the most important ones. The effectiveness of Soviet and third-world propaganda about Zionism being a form of racism. The myth that third-world dictatorships are somehow "left-wing." The use of anti-Zionism as a clever disguise for anti-Semitism. The fact that discrimination against a religion does not neatly fit into a traditional *class analysis* of society. The myth that most Jews are rich and powerful. The passage of time from the Holocaust, and the faltering of historical memory. The cynicism of international oil politics. The militaristic and repressive policies of Israel itself. The coziness of part of the American Jewish establishment with Nixon and Reagan. And a weakening of commitment to democracy by some American radicals, and the emergency of a double standard about human rights—i.e., William Kunstler saying openly: "I do not believe in public attacks on socialist countries, even where violations of human rights may occur." Kunstler favors quiet diplomacy to free the political prisoners in Vietnam, just as Kirkpatrick favors quiet diplomacy in Argentina.

Somehow we have arrived at a point in history where Jewish concerns are perceived to have a lesser claim on the conscience of the left than other groups, other nations, other nationalisms.

And let me emphasize that the current complex deadlock in the Middle East is not central to this article. Reasonable people of good will may differ about an ultimate solution that is fair to both Israel and the Palestinians. I stipulate that Israel is far from perfect. But my own identity as a Jew, and my sense of justice in the world, does not depend on, or derive from, Israel always being virtuous. All it requires is that Israel exist to work out its own problems. Certainly no one argues that the misdeeds of Pol Pot and Idi Amin are justification to liquidate Cambodia and Uganda as sovereign entities. And in the ethical measure of nations, Israel is still better than most.

The thing that troubles me about a part of the American left doesn't have an official sociological name. It's more than anti-Zionism, and different from traditional anti-Semitism. Its impact is often in omissions—the injustice not mentioned, the article not written, the petition not signed. It is often communicated in code words. But it is essentially a series of dual standards. It is a dual standard for the human rights of Jews in certain countries. It is a dual standard that questions Israel's right to exist by denying to Zionism the same moral legitimacy that is granted to every other expression of nationalism in the world. And it is an amnesia of conscience about the creation of Israel, and about the Holocaust, symbolized by Noam Chomsky writing an introduction to an insane, anti-Semitic book that alleges the Holocaust is a Zionist hoax. And by Jesse Jackson saying he is sick and tired of hearing about the Holocaust.

I am only talking about a minority of the left. There are many intellectual and political leaders on the left who, whatever their various shadings of belief, are shining examples of the single standard of democratic judgment.

Bella Abzug, who has lent her clear voice to every good cause in the world, spoke out forcefully and effectively against the Zionism-equals-racism myth at the International Women's Conference in Mexico City in 1975 and in Copenhagen in 1980. Anthony Lewis writes with the same eloquent passion about Jews in Argentina, Jews in Russia, and Palestinians on the West Bank. Nat Hentoff and Joan Baez are models of conscience who play no favorites among power blocs. The same can be said of Aryeh Neier, Roger Wilkins, Paul O'Dwyer, Ruth Messinger, Cesar Chavez, Elizabeth Holtzman, Andrew Young, I. F. Stone, Marcus Raskin, Julian Bond, and many others.

The apocalyptic pessimism of James Baldwin soured into ignorance and prejudice in an article he wrote for the *Nation*, September 29, 1979. Baldwin wrote the single most obscene sentence composed by a first-class writer since the days of Ezra Pound. He said: "The state of Israel was not created for the salvation of the Jews; it was created for the salvation of the Western interests."

Israel was created for the salvation of the Jews because of the genocide of six million of us! And the "Western interests" did everything in their power to prevent the creation of Israel!

Most of Harry Truman's advisers opposed the creation of Israel, including General George Marshall, Dean Acheson, Robert Lovett, and James Forrestal. Britain set up a blockade, and refugees from the Holocaust who tried to flee to Palestine were intercepted by the British and put behind barbed wire on Cyprus.

When the war began in 1948, Britain supplied arms to the Arabs, while the American State Department imposed an arms embargo in the Middle East, thereby denying guns to Israel.

In 1947, I. F. Stone celebrated the Passover seder in one of the British detention camps on Cyprus with the stateless Jewish refugees. Stone later published a moving reminiscence about the founding of Israel in his newsletter of February 6, 1956. There are a thousand possible sources to quote in rebuttal to Baldwin, but Izzy is my favorite.

"I had the privilege [Stone wrote] of seeing my people in some of the greatest moments of their long history—as they emerged from the hells of Auschwitz and Buchenwald—packed into the old freighters which served as the Mayflowers on the Mediterranean, fighting against odds which seemed overwhelming to establish a Jewish nation. . . .

"It is much too early to forget what happened with the rise of Hitler, the indifference of the State Department toward the prewar refugees, the shiploads the British Foreign Office turned away from Palestine in 1939–41, the hopeless who blew themselves up in mass suicide on the *Patria* and the *Struma,* the cruel farce of the Bermuda Conference at that very moment in 1943 when the remnants of the Warsaw ghetto were staging their uprising. Had there been the tiniest semblance of a Jewish state in Palestine, it could have saved many of those who later went to the crematoriums. . . .

"The Jews had no recourse in 1948 but to fight for their lives, and the war was stopped only when the Foreign Office and the

State Department suddenly realized that the Arabs were losing."

James Baldwin's distortion of history is mindless rhetoric, in the familiar code, to reinforce the Big Lie about Zionism being a form of racism. I've heard that Big Lie from Qaddafi, from Idi Amin, from Vanessa Redgrave, and from Amiri Baraka in the pages of the *Voice*. The ultimate purpose of that lie is to question Israel's right to exist, not to question a particular policy or administration. Modern Zionism is a reaction against the catastrophic racism of Hitler and the dying colonialism of Britain. To say that Zionism equals racism is to annul the meaning of language.

At the outset of the Iranian revolution, author and academic Richard Falk conscripted himself to become a publicist for Ayatollah Khomeini. Anyone is entitled to make a mistake. But Falk has persisted in propagandizing for the regime long after it was apparent that it suffered from many totalitarian defects, not the least of which was a paranoid, religious brand of anti-Semitism.

On February 16, 1979, Professor Falk published a *Times* Op-Ed column that charged the media has "defamed" Khomeini by, among other things, untruthfully accusing him of anti-Semitism. Subsequent events have proven Khomeini to be a Tyranis who has turned Iran into a theocratic madhouse.

But even back in February 1979 a careful scholar might have known better. In his book *Islamic Government*, published in 1970, Khomeini plainly stated his actual philosophy:

"It is our duty to shout at the top of our voices that the Jews and their foreign masters are plotting against Islam and are preparing the way for the Jews to rule over the entire planet. I greatly fear that by their own special methods, they will indeed realize their desired aims. It is because of our own weakness that we may wake up one morning and find a Jewish ruler dominating our country—God forbid!"

Falk must have been made aware of this book, and this quote, because it was part of a letter by Barry Youngerman published by the *Times* in rebuttal to Falk's Op-Ed column. Youngerman's letter also said:

"I fear that Professor Falk's failure to hear what Khomeini actually said is symptomatic of an increasing deafness to anti-Semitism among academics and liberal opinion makers that is beginning to frighten Jews like myself."

In the following months, the anti-Semitism of the Khomeini government became more and more flagrant. In May 1979, a Jewish businessman named Habib Eighanian was executed by a firing squad. His offense was "friendship with the enemies of God," the best evidence of which appears to be that he had purchased some land in Israel. For this, capital punishment was imposed by anonymous judges whose rulings are unappealable.

By the start of 1981, it was as clear as anything can be that the government in Iran was a horror on every count. There had been more than a thousand executions, after secret, sham trials bereft of due process. There had been persecution of many ethnic and religious minorities, especially Kurds and Jews; stonings and beatings to death of women accused of being liberated and Western; book burnings and newspaper closings; the violation of every conceivable liberty; plus the seizure of fifty-two American hostages.

But in an essay in the *Nation* (January 17, 1981) Professor Falk euphemistically called these "shortcomings," and said, "It's still too soon to pass judgment." Would he also say it is too soon to pass judgment on Duarte in El Salvador, or Botha in South Africa? Or Reagan?

Theodore Wilentz tried to slap Falk to his senses in a letter to the editor, and in his reply, Falk stated the left-wing hallucination that "one despotism has not replaced another," and urged we "refrain from premature condemnation."

In April of 1980, Amnesty International released a 203-page special report called *Prisoners of Conscience in the USSR: Their Treatment and Conditions.* The report describes more than a hundred prisoners of conscience confined to Soviet psychiatric hospitals for such crimes as "psychopathy with a tendency to litigation" and a "mania for reconstructing society."

Part of the Amnesty account makes Russia look like a giant theater of the absurd. One psychiatrist, in remanding a sane dissident to the mental ward, assures the court: "The absence of symptoms of an illness cannot prove the absence of the illness itself."

Or in another case, this exchange worthy of Pinter or Beckett:

DEFENSE COUNSEL: In what way was the behavior of Rozhedestvov delirious?

EXPERT: All his remarks and his behavior bore the mark of anti-Soviet
    views.
DEFENSE COUNSEL: What form did this delirium take?
EXPERT: He did not respond to correction.

Amnesty International's 1980 annual report surveying all nations condemned the Soviet Union on many counts, and observed: "Amnesty International still has not heard of a single case
in which a Soviet court has acquitted anyone charged with political or religious offenses."

Amnesty (which won the Nobel Prize in 1977) also reported
that it "believes that there are many more prisoners of conscience
than those of whom it knows. The real number is, however,
obscured by official censorship and secrecy regarding penal practices, and by the threat of retaliation against those who speak out
about political imprisonment."

Within this surreal and repressive system, which persecutes
many different minorities, there is a tremendous amount of anti-
Semitism, sanctioned by and promoted by the Soviet government.

Only a limited and decreasing number of Russia's three million Jews are permitted to emigrate to Israel each year. Jews who
do apply for visas risk rejection, harassment, loss of their jobs,
eviction from school, and arbitrary arrest. The irrationality of the
approval system has broken up many families, dividing parents
and children.

Every Soviet citizen has a passport with his nationality on it.
Only Jews have "Jew" stamped on theirs. The only other nation
that made religion into a nationality was Germany under Hitler.

The Soviet Academy of Sciences and several large publishing
houses have recently published anti-Semitic (not anti-Zionist)
books about a Jewish plot to control the world.

Refusenik Anatoly Shcharansky today is in solitary confine-
ment in the Perm Labor Camp, and his weight has dropped to
105 pounds. He has been denied all visitation rights for the entire
year of 1981—even his mother cannot see him. He is not even
permitted to have a photo of his wife Avital in his cell.
Shcharansky is serving three years in prison and ten years at hard
labor for "treason and espionage," although his only offense was

requesting a visa to emigrate to Israel. And then becoming an intellectual leader in making connections between political dissidents like Sakharov and nonpolitical Jews only seeking exit visas.

Are Russia's violations of human rights worse than South Korea's? Or Pakistan's? Or Brazil's?

The answer is: I don't know, and it doesn't matter. They are bad enough. They are bad enough to be protested by everyone who cares.

But some people who assert leadership on the left have, to my knowledge, almost never spoken out on the right of Russian Jews.

William Kunstler, who defends the civil liberties of almost every group in the world, including Mafia leaders, is silent about the worsening plight of Soviet Jewry.

There is only one way to conclude this essay. It is to quote the passage of Jacobo Timerman's testament that has come to hold the most meaning for me.

"The Holocaust will be understood not so much for the number of victims as for the magnitude of the silence. And what obsesses me most is the repetition of silence rather than the possibility of another Holocaust. . . .

"Whereas I, using my newspaper as a base, fought so that not even the slightest anti-Semitic trace should be left in silence, for the silence of the Jews is the sole indicator of the current presence of the Holocaust in the Jewish historical condition."
June 17, 1981

2

Power Corrupts and the Loss of Power Corrupts Absolutely: Going Bad

"The Case Against Koch" was written out of twenty years of familiarity. During the 1960s Koch was the lawyer for the *Village Voice*. We became friends. We had dinner together. We visited each other's homes.

As mayor, he was very popular, but I did not approve of the methods he employed to acquire his popularity. He colorfully scapegoated minorities in order to distract the middle class from the decline in police protection, subway service, housing, and education. He was a bully to the weak and a toady to the strong.

He provided a circus instead of services.

For years, most of the media, especially the publishers and editorial boards, loved Koch. Except for us at the *Village Voice*. We often disagreed with his policies and sometimes disputed his statistics. And since Koch treats all critics like enemies, his relationship with me, and the paper's other political writers, degenerated into a squalid public feud. The mayor called us "wackos" and "ideologues" at every opportunity. He publicly announced he would never give me, or Wayne Barrett, or Joe Conanson, an interview. He told Pete Hamill: "They should burn down the *Village Voice*—with Newfield in it!" (Hamill told this story at a public roast of me.)

But gradually our substantive criticisms of Koch's unequal treatment of blacks and Hispanics, of his tax giveaways to real estate developers, and of his political opportunism, were acknowledged, repeated, and improved on by others, especially by Jimmy Breslin and Earl Caldwell in the *Daily News*, and by Sydney Schanberg in *The New York Times*.

My investigative essay on Koch was published two weeks before his September 1982 primary for governor with Mario Cuomo. When the election campaign began, Koch was thirty-seven points ahead in the polls. He was being promoted as vice-presidential candidate in 1984. All three of New York's daily papers endorsed him over Cuomo. One week before the election, a *New York Post* poll, splashed on page one, had Koch eighteen points ahead.

But Cuomo scored an astonishing upset. He won partially because of an amazing, massive turnout among blacks, who voted for Cuomo by margins of 5 and 6 to 1 in some Brooklyn and Harlem districts. He won partially because he was an eloquent and inspiring candidate. And partially because Koch never developed a convincing rationalization for why he was running for governor of New York after saying for years that all he wanted out of life was three terms as mayor of New York City. By showing ambition and breaking his word, Koch overnight destroyed his uniqueness and credibility.

Now, after the gubernatorial election, the once invincible Koch seems vulnerable to political rejection as mayor in 1985. His popularity has waned. Our 1979 crank criticisms have become 1983 mainstream cliches. Koch's minimalist act has worn out. And I think I saw it early because I know the man's character from twenty years of intimate observation. The lessons I took from all this are the relevance of character to the making of public policy. Of not backing down when a popular mayor starts a public brawl. And the wisdom of that popular expression: "What goes around, comes around."

The piece on Carol Bellamy was difficult to write. I respected several members of her staff enormously. I had previously written favorably about her. Many women I knew identified with her and admired her, without knowing too many specific details of her public records.

But I felt a professional obligation to update my opinion of her, which had changed. And I felt the realist's urge to correct the romantic illusions about her.

I also felt guilty that I had participated in the *Voice*'s decision to endorse her, rather than Paul O'Dwyer, in the election for council president in 1977. I discovered that my political judgment was fallible, that I had given in to my own need for a politician to believe in. So the essay on Bellamy was a matter of squaring accounts, of admitting a mistake, and of keeping my own streak of romanticism under control. The piece was a quarrel with myself.

The first time I met Congressman John Murphy was in 1967 and he called me a "commie sympathizer." The occasion was a debate about the Vietnam war on the Barry Gray radio program. I made a mental note to remember John Murphy.

More than ten years later a woman wrote me claiming that someone on Murphy's staff had asked for a bribe in exchange for a constituent favor. I could never verify the allegation, but it started me digging into the tangled business dealings of the powerful congressman—chairman of the Maritime Committee, senior member of the New York City delegation.

My front page exposé on John Murphy was published in September of 1979. Murphy—a warrior by instinct—counterattacked immediately. He bought a two-page advertisement in the *Voice* to deny all. And on October 18, 1979, he met with a high official of the Justice Department in the office of his lawyer, to request a federal investigation into my sources, claiming I was getting confidential grand jury information in violation of the law.

This October 18 meeting required the cool arrogance Murphy possessed in abundance. I say this because Murphy had already agreed to have a secret meeting two days later at JFK Airport, with what turned out to be the undercover agents of Abscam. Although I did not know it at the time, Murphy accepted a $50,000 cash bribe on October 20, 1979—less than a month after my exposé of him was published, and less than forty-eight hours after he accused me of a crime, in the privacy of his attorney's office.

Murphy went to trial in November of 1980, along with Representative Frank Thompson. And to the shock of his many admirers, John Murphy, the fearless soldier who won the Purple Heart in Korea, refused to take the stand in his own defense. On December 3, 1980, a jury found him guilty on three felony counts after deliberating for twenty-two hours. He was sentenced to three years in prison. On July 15, 1983, Murphy entered the federal prison in Danbury, Connecticut.

Of all the Abscam defendants, the government's videotapes revealed Murphy to be the slickest and the smartest. He never touched the money; he let his bagman carry the suitcase. And he was the only congressman cunning enough to grow suspicious of the whole scenario in his final meeting with the FBI undercover team. He made exculpatory comments, but they seemed cynical, and without authentic feeling or conviction in his eyes. He seemed to suspect a hidden audio microphone, but not a secret video camera.

Murphy reminds me of the brave hero cop who turns bad. With his fortunate face, war medals, and agile mind, Murphy had the potential to become senator or governor. But somewhere along the way, money became his god, and he started to apply his large capacities to wayward ends.

THE CASE AGAINST KOCH

I have known Ed Koch for more than twenty years. I was a volunteer in his 1962 campaign for the assembly—the only election he ever lost. Koch was the attorney for the *Village Voice* for many years, and he used to hang out in our old offices on Sheridan Square. I wrote at least a dozen favorable articles about Koch during the 1960s, praising in particular his devotion to civil liberties, tenants' rights, and mass transportation. I've been to his home and he has been to mine. We shared similar tastes in Italian restaurants and in popular music (Paul Simon and Joan Baez). When Representative Koch wanted to testify about corruption in the nursing home industry in 1975, he came to my home, and I gave him my files on Bernard Bergman to take away and study. I think I understand Ed Koch at least as well as any writer.

Over the years I have watched Ed Koch gradually change, watched him accommodate to wealth, political fashion, and looser ethics.

The man who launched his reform career by defeating Carmine DeSapio has become master of the system of insider favors that DeSapio merely came to symbolize because of his dark glasses. The man who more than once told me that "Roy Cohn is the most vile person in New York" this year accepted a $1000 campaign contribution from Cohn's law firm.

In the early 1970s, Koch would regularly lash out at landlords and bankers as "special interests"; last October, when he spoke to a meeting of national Democrats in Baltimore, Koch warned the party against enslavement to "special interests" he oddly defined as "environmental groups and organizations for the handicapped."

Ed Koch, who once risked his career to stop the Lower Manhattan Expressway, has become the champion of an even more wasteful and damaging highway. Ed Koch, who once had a 100 percent voting record according to the AFL-CIO, has become a union baiter and a union buster. Ed Koch, who campaigned for Robert Kennedy in 1968, helped to elect Ronald Reagan and Alfonse D'Amato in 1980. Ed Koch, who urged the creation of national commercial rent controls in 1971, now opposes Ruth Messinger's legislation to create commercial rent controls in New York City.

The man who marched with me from Selma to Montgomery in 1965 now says, "My experience with blacks is that they're basically anti-Semitic," although he has no close black friends on which to base his bigoted generalization. The man who once made it a point to denounce "poverty pimps" has become the political ally and benefactor of Ramon Velez and Joe Galiber, giving them jobs, city contracts, and even buying landfill cover dirt from a company owned by Galiber and convicted hoodlum Billy the Butcher Masselli. The man who promised in 1977 to appoint one black deputy mayor and one Hispanic deputy mayor now says *racial* quotas are "ultraliberal stupidity," although he favors *geographical* quotas this year for the Democratic state ticket.

The reasons Ed Koch changed are not my province. It would probably take a psychiatrist to make sense out of them. My interest is only in the concrete public consequences of these changes.

I could offer a hundred arguments why Ed Koch should not be elected governor. He would execute people. He would try to build Westway. He would give Stanley Friedman and his law partner Roy Cohn more control over the machinery of state government. He would become a neoconservative mole pulling the national Democratic party to the right.

But here I will limit my case against Koch to the four systemic reasons that go to the root of his disqualification for higher office: his failure to deliver city services, his essential Republicanism, his divisive and devious methods of leadership, and the extraordinary amount of money he has collected from special interests that do business with the city, thus distorting Koch's understanding of the public interest. Measuring the quality of municipal services is more than impressionistic but less than scientific. Experts differ over methodology and which statistics are the most meaningful. Does the number of arrests per officer tell more about the efficiency of police work, or does the total number of crimes reported reveal more? How do you measure the quality of care in a hospital emergency room? How do you determine what the closing of Sydenham Hospital has meant to life in Harlem? Do reading scores, or truancy rates, or teacher-pupil ratios best illuminate the quality of public education?

My personal experience and observation, supported by a February 1982 study made by the business-oriented Citizens Budget Commission, is that under Ed Koch the quality of life has gotten worse, and that most city services have deteriorated, most acutely mass transit and police protection.

Most of the Koch commissioners in high visibility agencies are able administrators. But they personally can't compensate for an insufficient number of subway maintenance employees, an insufficient number of doctors and nurses. If you asked most New Yorkers Ronald Reagan's simple question of 1980—"Are you better off today than four years ago?"—the answer would have to be No.

The Citizens Budget Commission is a credible, business-ori-
ented civic watchdog. Its board of trustees includes bankers like
E. Virgil Conway and John Larsen, realtors like Alton Marshal
and Alan Tishman, and investment managers like Charles Agee
Atkins (an $18,000 contributor to Koch). The chairman of the
CBC board is banker Lawrence Huntington.

In February of 1982 this fiscally conservative research organization released the first of a series of reports monitoring the
delivery of city services. The conclusion of the forty-five-page
CBC analysis was that the following services have gotten worse
under Mayor Koch:

police protection
subways
transit police
fire protection
street cleaning
ambulance response time
hospital efficiency

The only services that showed improvement between 1978 and
1981 were refuse collection, corrections, and education in grades
nine to twelve.

The study had been approved by the CBC's trustees in advance of public release. City officials had been shown drafts of the
study in advance and suggested changes. But when the report
generated a few newspaper headlines, Deputy Mayor Nat Leventhal claimed the authors of the report were biased and the report
contained "gross inaccuracies." After an exchange of correspon-
dence, Leventhal retracted his bias charge when he could only
substantiate two nonmaterial errors in the report, one of which
originated in the city's own data.

In the area of police protection, the budget commission's
study concluded that, during the Koch years of 1978 to 1981, the
felony arrest rate dropped 28.3 percent, and the felony clearance
rate of crimes solved fell by 20.6 percent. The report went on to
say: "The efficiency of law enforcement activity has worsened.
. . . A measure of law enforcement efficiency, namely annual
arrests per uniformed employee, fell 10.1 percent."

The raw statistics supplied to the *Voice* by the New York City

Police Department document a rise in crime in each year Koch
has been mayor: 115,000 more crimes were reported in 1981 than
in 1978. Murders have increased from 1504 in 1978 to 1826 in
1981; robberies have increased from 74,029 in 1978 to 104,495
in 1981; auto thefts have increased from 83,112 in 1978 to
104,706 last year; burglaries rose from 164,447 in 1978 to 205,825
last year. Rape and arson also went up in 1981.

And this crime increase took place during a period of population decrease.

A significant factor in the crime rise during the Koch years has
been the underfunding of the Police Department. As Arthur
Browne and Mark Lieberman wrote in the *Daily News* of April
20, 1982: "Where crime is concerned, Mayor Koch does not
always put his money where his mouth is.

"While Koch has loudly proclaimed the city's record-breaking
crime wave as his No. 1 priority, he actually cut the police department's share of the dollars New Yorkers pay in taxes.

"According to state figures, if Koch had kept the police share
of his budget constant, the city could have hired nearly twelve
hundred more cops to fight the crime wave that began the year
after he took office and continues today."

The Browne-Lieberman investigative report went on to point
out that candidate Koch in 1977 promised again and again to
increase the number of cops on daily patrol. On the day Koch was
inaugurated as mayor, the department had an average of 6636
cops on patrol. In March of this year, the average daily patrol
strength had dwindled to 6079—the lowest in the city's history.

The FBI's Uniform Crime Report, made public last month,
reveals that serious crime increased in New York City during
1981, *while it was dropping by 2 percent in the rest of the country.*
This deviation from the national trend is perhaps the most indict-
ing statistic of all.

In this election year, the Koch administration is belatedly
hiring 2300 new cops, and the crime rate has dipped in the last
six months. The crucial fact, however, is that it is the Board of
Estimate and City Council—not Koch—who deserve the credit
for these 2300 new cops, although Koch is typically trying to steal
the credit. Koch originally proposed a budget with enough funds
to hire only 1300 rookie cops. The Board of Estimate and City

Council forced Koch to accept the additional funds for a thousand extra police. Nevertheless, because of retirements and other forms of attrition, the police department this month has fewer cops on patrol than on the day Koch became mayor.

According to Special Deputy State Comptroller Sidney Schwartz, the Koch administration allocated to the police department $29 million less in city tax dollars between 1979 and 1981. That money would have meant 1170 new cops.

One definition of a demagogue might be: a politician who shortchanges the police, and then goes to a senior citizen center to make a tough speech about the electric chair and work camps.

It is hardly a secret that subway service has gone from crummy to calamitous under Koch. The Transit Authority's own published statistics document the daily inhuman grind for 1.5 million riders. Late trains have increased from 35,000 in 1978 to 110,000 in 1981. Collisions and derailments have jumped from 14 in 1978 to 21 in 1981. Serious breakdowns en route have escalated from 13,000 in 1978 to 37,000 in 1981. Track fires have more than doubled, from 2400 in 1978 to 5500 last year. Crime—including murder, assault, and robbery—has nearly doubled on the subways, while the transit police force, whose annual budget is under direct control of the mayor, has diminished from 3600 in 1976 to 2600 this year. And while service, safety, and reliability have all gotten worse, the transit fare has gone from 60 cents to 75 cents.

The Citizens Budget Commission study confirms this data, pointing out that total subway ridership has declined, rush hour performance has declined, and the efficiency of the transit police (felony arrests per officer) has declined 26 percent between 1978 and 1981.

And just this month, MTA vice-chairman Daniel Scannell conceded in a memorandum that subway service has gotten even worse during the last two months, with more subway cars breaking down and interrupting service than ever before. Subway cars are now breaking down on an average of every 7400 miles. This is a steady decline from the 8100-mile mark of December 1981.

Koch has gone through a series of evasive public relations defenses about city services. For several years he claimed they really weren't so bad. Then he began to invent scapegoats. He blamed the transit union for the collapse of subway service. He

blamed "soft judges" for the rise in crime, although he appointed
the judge who decided a sentence on the flip of a coin. Then Koch
declared crime was his top priority. Then he declared the subways
his top priority. Then, during his reelection campaign in 1981,
he pledged that the improvement of services would be the four-
year preoccupation of his second term, a pledge he now seeks to
evade.

But there was a memorable moment on television last year
when Koch, under resourceful questioning by Bill Moyers, confessed the truth about services. I quote from the official transcript
of the interview, aired by PBS on January 5, 1981.

MOYERS: Are the poor better off today than they were three years ago?
KOCH: Are the middle class better than they were three years ago?
MOYERS: No. Are they?
KOCH: And therefore—
MOYERS: Neither is, then:
KOCH: Neither. Of course not.

Since the summer of 1980, Ed Koch has been more of a
Republican than a Democrat. Prior to 1980, Koch had endorsed
Republican John Lindsay for mayor in 1965, which was appropriate; and he had endorsed State Senator John Marchi for reelection in 1978, which was understandable as an isolated judgment.

But in the summer of 1980, in the midst of a campaign for
president, Koch—who understands symbolism—testified before
the Republican party's national platform committee. Koch was a
big hit with the party of Reaganomics.

After Koch testified, Representative Trent Lott, a right-wing
budget slasher from Mississippi, invited Koch to rejoin him in
Congress because "You're singing our song." Bill Brock, the Re-
publican national chairman, praised Koch's ideas, and told him:
"You have made the most eloquent argument for a Republican
Congress that I have ever heard."

Late in September of 1980, the mayor held a City Hall press
conference with Republican senate candidate Alfonse D'Amato,
then just beginning to close the gap against Elizabeth Holtzman
in a close election. Koch hugged D'Amato for the cameras, and

all the television tape and newspaper photos gave D'Amato new legitimacy with Jewish voters. The next day, in one of his most biting columns, Murray Kempton wrote:

"There is something about the mayor's posture in these encounters that suggests less the prudent man of affairs than the enthusiastic trembling toward being born again. His meeting with D'Amato went beyond detente to embrace fraternity. . . . No one who listened to this duet has any cause to think there was any difference between them. But oughtn't there to be? Koch did not say one word that indicated he had any more sympathy than D'Amato for the concept that government has a special duty to the deprived. Instead, he summoned his widest smile when the Republican-Conservative candidate expressed his pleasure at being in the company of a twin fiscal conservative. . . .

"I could not care less whether Koch does his duty to the Democratic party. But all of us ought to care whether he does his duty to our city.

"A great part of that duty is to think of its worse-cheated and sorely deprived citizens with the compassion he so rarely, rather than the resentment he so frequently shows. He ought to be crying out against the national Democratic and Republican parties in the name of our abandoned children; instead he alternately beams with bi-partisan benevolence upon both of them."

Alfonse D'Amato, of course, went on to nose out Liz Holtzman by less than 1 percent, and go to Washington, where he has voted for massive budget cuts in mass transit, school lunches, health care, student loans, legal services, summer jobs for teenagers, day care, and Social Security.

On October 17, 1980, Koch participated in a similar ritual with Ronald Reagan. With more than a hundred local and national reporters standing on the lawn at Gracie Mansion, Koch said that he "preferred Mr. Reagan's policies on the Middle East to those of the President." Another misleading message to Jewish voters that another right-winger was kosher. And as recently as February 17, 1982, Koch said, "I have never regretted my decision to brief Mr. Reagan during the campaign." The grateful president reciprocated with the famous *New York Post* headline of March 24, 1982: "PREZ LIKES ED FOR GOV."

The zenith of Koch's Republicanism came last year, when he

sought and received the Republican party's official endorsement
for mayor. Along the way he picked up well-earned endorsements
from voodoo economist Jack Kemp, John Calandra, Al D'Amato,
William Simon, and Richard Nixon. Nixon's encomium was be-
stowed when Koch personally attended a gala Republican party
fundraiser last year at Lincoln Center. The Unindicted Cocon-
spirator said of Koch: "He's pretty much of a shoo-in, and de-
serves to be."

The $300,000 raised at this event was used to subsidize cam-
paigns by Republicans running against Democrats for the state
legislature, including rural, upstate Republicans opposed to economic assistance to New York City. The funds were also used to
preserve a Republican majority in the state senate, which is also
harmful to the interests of New York City.

Despite all this history, Ed Koch, with a straight face, is now
charging Mario Cuomo with treason to the Democratic party,
because Cuomo has accepted the Liberal party line on the bal-
lot.

But the essential issue here, as Murray Kempton wrote, is not
loyalty to the Democratic party, because as an institution it does
not merit much loyalty. The essential issue is that Koch gives aid
and comfort to the enemies of New York City, that Koch plays
a political game with the miscreants (Reagan, Kemp, D'Amato)
who, along with the mayor himself, are the cause of our present
misfortune.

Ed Koch's methods of leadership include abuse, bullying,
scapegoating, code words, polarization, and breaking his word. All
this contaminates the democratic polity. There is no question that
Koch has been remarkably successful with this style of leadership.
But it has created divisions and resentments beneath the surface
that are unhealthy. A price is paid in the public's disillusionment
with government when Koch misleads us on such basic questions
as completing his current term as mayor, or giving every assurance
that he would not build Westway. A bill will come due in this city
some day because of the way Koch has ill-served and insulted
black communities during his administration.

There are countless examples of Koch's flip-flops on public
policy questions, where he takes one position and then senses
some quick political advantage and changes sides. It is almost as

if Koch keeps a Garth poll where his conscience ought to be, so he can tell people what they want to hear, even before they can express themselves.

A few recent Koch flip-flops include:

the surtax on suburban commuters (yes to no)
the nuclear freeze movement (no to yes)
Mario Biaggi's $500 million "super-fund" to combat crime (no to yes)
construction on parkland at Tudor City (yes to no)
the transfer of control over Rikers Island prison to the state (yes to no)
the 1980 subway fare increase to 75 cents (no to yes)
Carol Bellamy ("pain in the ass" to worthy successor)

No politician, no candidate, ever made a more binding covenant with the voters than Ed Koch made over Westway. During the 1977 campaign for mayor, dozens of audiences heard Koch promise to kill Westway, if they would only vote for him. On October 26, 1977, Koch even put it in writing, in a letter to then state commissioner of environmental conservation, Peter Berle. Koch wrote: "I have concluded that the Westway proposal is an economic and environmental disaster. You know the reasons, and I need not outline them." Two days later, *The New York Times* carried a front-page story that quoted Koch as vowing "Westway will never be built."

But Koch eventually switched sides, and is still pushing Westway, despite a federal judge enjoining all funding, nullifying all approvals, and accusing the highway's planners of fraud and cover-up. After Westway, Koch is simply not believable in any guarantee he might make about his future conduct. Will he abolish rent control? Will he back the Republican candidate for president in 1984? We can't be sure. His present words are no guide to his future actions.

In September 1979, *The New Yorker* published Ken Auletta's two-part profile of Koch. Koch gave Auletta access to the oral history tapes he had placed under seal at Columbia University. And one of the most revealing quotes Auletta used from these archives was Koch saying about himself: "I always like to tweak people if I can, especially if I don't like them. There is something that is really vicious in me."

And so there is. It is a quality that is unattractive in a friend, but dangerous in a political leader who tends to personalize all disagreements, who sees skeptics as enemies. Koch uses his power to try to hurt people less powerful than himself, people who can't defend themselves.

Koch is a bully to the weak, but a toady to the strong. When he disagreed with Jimmy Carter's Middle East policy, he did not directly challenge the president. He attacked his subordinates, two of whom just happened to be black—Andrew Young and Donald McHenry. When Koch articulated his distaste for the Liberal party, he didn't attack Governor Carey, who has had great influence over the party, or attack Raymond Harding, who controls the party; he attacked Reverend Donald Harrington as "slime," knowing full well that Harrington is merely a figurehead. In last year's aborted City Council elections, Koch did not try to use his popularity in a constructive way to encourage and endorse candidates of quality; he used it destructively, negatively, to punish those council members he did not like personally—Susan Alter, Abe Gerges, and Miriam Friedlander. He endorsed their inferior challengers while doing nothing to rid the council of its senior drones, an effort that would have served a higher civic purpose than revenge.

Koch is also afflicted with a terminal case of the Arrogance of Power, also known as Yertle the Turtle syndrome.

Last year, professors Raymond Horton and Charles Brecher published their annual volume on municipal priorities, and mildly criticized the decline in some services and the treatment of the poor. Koch reacted by publicly attacking the motives of the professors and boycotting the conference on city affairs the two academics conduct annually at Arden House. Koch then ordered all his commissioners, who had already accepted invitations to speak at the conference, to cancel them.

In July of 1982 the *Daily News* caught Koch using Police Department helicopters (the city only has six) and police bodyguards to speed him to gubernatorial campaign appearances at taxpayer expense. Only after the *News* embarrassed Koch did the mayor's campaign finance committee reimburse the city treasury for $19,000 in travel expenses. And ever since this story, Koch has been complaining that the *News* is biased and "out to get me with a series of hatchet jobs."

There obviously is "something really vicious" within Ed Koch, as he seems to boast in his oral history memoir. The public record is filled with his false and petty remarks about people who differ with him. He seems particularly cruel to women, from calling Carol Bellamy "a horror show," to red-baiting Bella Abzug and Jane Fonda in the *Playboy* interview, to his attacks on Liz Holtzman and Ruth Messinger, to his bizarre remarks about Andy Logan in the August 23, 1982, *New York* magazine: "She's purely vicious. I think I inhabit her dreams." (Andy Logan is the shy, polite City Hall writer for *The New Yorker*.)

This nation, and this city, have suffered from the consequences of leaders who have vast political gifts, and vast gifts as communicators, but who abuse their power owing to some personality defect. The more power Ed Koch acquires, the more he will use it to express the demons within that make him the way he is.

Ed Koch, Mario Cuomo, and Lewis Lehrman have all spent large sums of money in this election. But there are some differences, since Koch has gotten such a large proportion of his money from landlords, bankers, and law firms that do business with the city.

Lehrman has spent $2.6 million of his own money. We may resent the unfair advantage of Lehrman's private fortune, but we should also acknowledge that rich candidates are also less dependent on campaign money from venal interests seeking a quid pro quo. This financial independence, for example, has probably made it easier for Lehrman to oppose both Westway and Lincoln West.

The single largest source of funds to Mario Cuomo's campaign has been private sector labor unions. Cuomo has received $18,000 from each of these large unions: the ILGWU, the Amalgamated Clothing and Textile Workers, the Seafarers International Union, the International Brotherhood of Electrical Workers, and the Communications Workers of America (CWA).

But private sector unions have a limited dependency on government, less than public employee unions that negotiate contracts, and much less than real estate companies that are sometimes totally dependent on government subsidies, abatements, approvals, variances, and assessments. Moreover, a union seeking higher wages for its members should not be equated with a landlord seeking more profits for himself.

Another difference is the method Koch has used to raise his $2.7 million this year. Several of Koch's large donors have told me the same story. They were approached for contributions, and although they don't like Koch, they were afraid not to contribute because they were reminded that even if he loses, Koch will still be mayor, and Koch will still have a vindictive mentality.

Up until this year I had believed—and had written—that Koch's personal probity was beyond question. But his fund-raising operation in this election raises grave doubts about his ethical standards.

How can Koch accept $18,500 in contributions from the developers of Lincoln West, and then say there is nothing wrong with his casting the deciding vote next week to build the $1 billion luxury development that every elected official on the West Side is opposed to? What would the press say, and what would the public think, if a judge accepted $18,500 from one party to a lawsuit, and then claimed that it won't affect his judgment on the case?

In going over Koch's list of contributors, I have been able to identify $600,000 from individuals, law firms, and companies that do business with the city, contributors that Koch has benefited or can benefit, even if he loses the race for governor. All these contributions give the appearance of a conflict of interest, of wealth buying power to perpetuate wealth.

The appropriate remedy to this insidious process should be public financing of elections, or else strict legal limits on the amounts of money individuals can contribute. Mario Cuomo has endorsed a $500 limitation on contributions for statewide office, and a $2 million spending cap which would limit the amount of personal wealth a candidate like Lehrman could use.

The old Ed Koch favored campaign finance reform, just as the old Ed Koch favored civil rights, protecting the environment, and the funding of mass transit ahead of highways. But the new Ed Koch is opposed to public financing of elections, or to any curbs on the size of contributions. Koch's remedy to the scandal of big money dominating elected government is shorter election seasons. This is a silly solution, impossible to legislate, regulate, or enforce.

Ed Koch is our first minimalist politician. He is a magician with one trick, a play with one joke. Koch's genius as a political leader has been his capacity to change with the fashions, to flip-flop with the wind. This agility, this counterfeit candor, has allowed him to say whatever the middle class has wanted to hear at a particular moment in time, regardless of past beliefs or future intentions.

But there is an inevitable down side to this kind of oral, media politics. A politician, even one so verbal as Koch, cannot get away with the strategy indefinitely. At some point, maybe this year, maybe next year, strength becomes weakness, as opportunism finally begins to erode credibility.

At some point, after enough seasons of violated promises and undelivered services, cleverness eventually turns into arrogance, macho becomes divisiveness, and candor curdles into deceit.
September 14, 1982

BELLAMY SINKING

The rise, fall, and vaporization of Carol Bellamy as a liberal meteor is now nearly complete. I say this with a mixture of contrition and regret since I was among those most blinded by the brilliance of her rise. And I say this with a sense of loss—and even tragedy—because her potential has been annulled by a self-inflicted wound. Carol Bellamy seems to have lost her way not out of any venality or scheming defection, but rather out of some inner loss of identity and failure of nerve. At age forty-one, she no longer seems to know who she is, or what she really thinks, or where she comes from.

What prompts these reflections is the fact, not previously publicized, that Carol Bellamy voted for a resolution supporting a subminimum wage for teenagers at the conference of the National League of Cities last month in Washington. Bellamy voted for this antilabor resolution despite a passionate speech against it by black Detroit Councilwoman Erma Henderson, and despite a subcommittee recommendation backed by liberal Minneapolis Mayor Don Fraser and Manhattan Councilwoman Ruth Messinger against diluting the minimum wage law.

The resolution that Bellamy supported at this national conference of urban leaders differs only in degree and detail from Ronald Reagan's proposal; the Bellamy resolution applies the subminimum wage only to youths aged fourteen to eighteen (instead of fourteen to twenty-two), and it limits the exploitive experiment to the summer months. But probably all union activists would agree with Jan Pierce of CWA, who says: "Any compromise that weakens the minimum wage law, for any category of workers, is unconscionable."

The minimum wage issue is so fundamental to the rights of labor it must have required a total suspension of sense for Bellamy to behave the way she did. Unless she thought she could do it discreetly in Washington, before a national constituency of her peers, and that word of the deed would not filter back to her labor and liberal allies in New York. Actually, six days after her performance at the National League of Cities, Bellamy spoke to a conference of labor union women who innocently applauded her as she scolded Reaganomics.

And that is the disturbing contradiction of Carol Bellamy, who seems trapped between her humanitarian rhetoric and her balanced budget/middle-class instincts. On some issues, like foster care, food stamps, or teenage pregnancies, Bellamy can be convincing and persistent. But time after time, when the crunch comes on the difficult issues of racial and economic justice, she will publicly agonize in indecision, and then try to invent some procedural compromise that begs the question, and then, in the end, she will bend to power, and disappoint her old friends.

Bellamy cast the deciding vote in February of 1979 that killed the Charlotte Street low-income housing project in the South Bronx. But she killed it with a trembling voice, and after having voted in favor of the project a few months earlier. She campaigned for Ed Koch for governor last year, but she seemed guilty and uncomfortable doing it. She procrastinated until after midnight, and then, looking vulnerable, voted to build the luxury, high-rise development—Lincoln West—which has been temporarily halted by the state courts. She waited till the last minute in 1981 and then endorsed Stanley Simon over Ismael Betancourt and Andrew Stein over David Dinkins, thus helping to guarantee an all-white Board of Estimate in a 50 percent nonwhite city.

Carol Bellamy acts like she knows right from wrong, but she lacks the courage of her rhetoric.

The real motive behind these disappointing actions and others to be described is unknowable to any journalist. In Bellamy's case these disappointments are all the more painful because she was elected in 1977 on a surge of generational and feminist hopes and liberal endorsements. Despite Paul O'Dwyer's lifetime as a rebel, Bellamy beat him because Victor Gotbaum, *The New York Times*, the *Village Voice*, Stanley Fink, Mary Ann Krupsak, Fred Ohrenstein, Bob Abrams, Carl McCall, and Robert Steingut all believed her promises of political independence from the mayor, and endorsed her during the run-off with O'Dwyer.

The bulk of Bellamy's disappointing decisions falls in three broad categories: her insensitivity to fair representation by blacks and Hispanics in elected office; her loss of political independence to both the mayor and to the Brooklyn clubhouse machine; and her elitist priorities in terms of land use, development, and housing.

When a public policy question is posed in abstract generalities, Bellamy will often take a liberal position on issues involving racial equality. But when the issue has moved from the abstract to the concrete, from easy rhetoric to hard decision, Bellamy has repeatedly failed to endorse qualified minority candidates when she has been offered the opportunity to help elect to public office people who would actually implement her own public policy generalities.

In 1981, when Wayne Barrett and I interviewed Bellamy

about her de facto support for an all-white Board of Estimate, she offered inconsistent logic to justify her simultaneous endorsements of Stein and Simon. She defended her backing for Simon by saying that Simon had voted for her proposals to reform the city's foster care programs, which was true. They were good reforms and Bellamy had worked hard to pass them. But it was Stein whose last-minute betrayal of Bellamy caused the narrow defeat of her foster care program by the Board of Estimate.

Bellamy explained that she endorsed Stein over Dinkins in the general election, after remaining neutral during the primary, because she "believed deeply" in the principle of party loyalty and discipline. But this excuse also was bereft of credibility, since in 1977 Bellamy had violated party loyalty to endorse Robert Wagner Jr. on the Liberal Party line against the same Andrew Stein.

In July of 1981, Wayne Barrett was a member of a panel of journalists that interviewed Bellamy on ABC-TV's "Eyewitness News Conference," and Barrett pressed Bellamy on the question of her racial insensitivity. Bellamy avoided criticizing the all-white Board of Estimate by saying she preferred not to discuss "percentages" of racial or ethnic groups. She would not object to zero percent. She seemed unusually defensive and implicitly hostile to the concept of affirmative action, which she is not.

Bellamy also said she was "satisfied" with the minority representation on her own staff, which at the time was one black and no Latins among the top twelve policymaking positions. Today, there is one black and one Latin among Bellamy's top fifteen staffers—not one in her inner circle of advisers.

Bellamy is certainly *not* racially prejudiced, as I am convinced Mayor Koch is. She does *not* intentionally engage in polarization or divisiveness. She did endorse Bruce Wright for Civil Court in 1980, and she did endorse Carl McCall for lieutenant governor in 1982.

Bellamy's pattern of endorsing mediocre whites over qualified minorities is rather, I suspect, a complicated product of intellectual confusion, personal isolation from minorities, and a deepening entanglement with the odious Harold Fisher faction of the Brooklyn machine. (Fisher arranged Bellamy's appointment to the MTA board.) It is useful to recall that in Brooklyn primaries Bellamy not only opposed Roger Green and Bernard Gifford; she also refused to endorse her own close friend and dedicated supporter, Virginia Apuzzo, when she ran against Assemblyman Strelzin in 1978. And in 1981, Bellamy endorsed the reactionary Noach Dear against Susan Alter, a woman City Council incumbent with a generally progressive and independent voting record. Dear and Strelzin were backed by Harold Fisher.

The main theme of Bellamy's winning 1977 campaign was political purity and independence. She campaigned on the notion that Paul O'Dwyer was too old and too cozy with Mayor Beame, and that she, as a "child of the sixties," would provide a more assertive and vigorous example.

Probably the most dramatic case study of Bellamy's failed promise of independence was her early and enthusiastic campaigning for Mayor Koch against Mario Cuomo in last year's Democratic primary for governor. Bellamy's embrace of Koch seemed transparently opportunistic on several counts. First, she had made her real views about Koch clear the previous year by never endorsing Koch in his primary against Frank Barbaro. Second, Koch had made *his* real views about Bellamy clear when he called her a "horror show" and "a pain in the ass." But Bellamy would become mayor if Koch beat Cuomo, so Bellamy sacrificed principle—and pride—and embraced the man who had humiliated her in print.

But Bellamy did more than endorse a candidate with whom she disagreed on such basic matters as the death penalty and Westway. She campaigned for him. She urged her staff to volunteer for his campaign. She personally went to the offices of *El Diario*, the Spanish language daily, to argue (successfully) for the paper to endorse Koch. The nadir of lost self-respect came on election night. With the raw vote already suggesting a Cuomo upset, a tense Bellamy went on live television to deny reality and to predict that Koch would yet prevail. It was an embarrassing public moment of wish-fulfillment.

Bellamy's embrace of Koch is at least understandable at some level. She compromised in order to gain something substantial for herself. It was a Faustian bargain.

But her neutrality in the reelection of City Council Majority Leader Tom Cuite was not even understandable in terms of self-interest. It was both dishonorable and stupid politics.

I have a minimum expectation of liberal politicians. All I require is that they have at least one or two ideas or issues that they really believe in at some human level and will risk their office for. I assume they will compromise on most other issues. I always felt that John Lindsay, in his gut, believed in black equality and civil liberties, whatever the political price. I always felt that George McGovern opposed the Vietnam war with all his being. I have seen Mario Cuomo lose an election for mayor because he had such profound legal/moral/religious objections to the electric chair. I know that Bella Abzug's commitment to disarmament, equal rights for women, and civil liberties is unbreakable.

And whatever misgivings I was developing about Carol Bellamy, I thought, until last September, that she too had some bottom-line beliefs for which she would be willing to risk some loss of personal popularity. I thought that her commitment to feminism and gay rights was her bottom line. That whatever else she did, these were real principles with her, and that nothing could get her to violate them because she cared about them at a level beyond routine politics.

In last year's primary, Steve DiBrienza challenged Tom Cuite. Cuite has singlehandedly caused the defeat of the gay rights bill for nearly a decade. And Cuite is opposed to abortion and last year was endorsed by the Right-to-Life party, as well as running in the Democratic primary. His defeat would have done much to further the two causes I thought Carol Bellamy had a special faith in.

But Carol Bellamy never endorsed Steve DiBrienza. All her oldest friends in reform politics were supporting DiBrienza, and they all pleaded for her endorsement, which could have been decisive in that district. Assemblywoman Eileen Dugan asked. Assemblyman Joe Ferris asked. These were the friends who had helped elect Bellamy to the state senate in 1972 by 360 votes.

But she thought she was going to be mayor, and all her future friends were supporting Tom Cuite—future friends like Ed Koch, Harold Fisher, the *New York Post,* and Howard Golden.

So Bellamy rejected her own past and remained silent; Cuite won by 500 votes; and the gay rights bill lost again this year.

Now I understand there is no issue on earth for which Carol Bellamy will choose conscience over power.

Charlotte Street in the south Bronx became a synonym for

urban desolation because Jimmy Carter stood on that windswept moonscape in 1977 and made a solemn promise of reconstruction. On February 8, 1979, the Board of Estimate rejected a $1.5 billion housing development plan to be constructed on the wasteland where Carter had stood. The plan was not perfect, but no plan is ever perfect. It was a good plan and it would have helped thousands of poor people. It would have brought millions of federal dollars into the south Bronx. And it was an important symbol of hope to millions of people. The Charlotte Street plan died when five members of the Board of Estimate voted "no." Carol Bellamy was one of the five. If she had voted in the affirmative, the plan would have passed six to five. (The other negative votes were cast by Harrison Goldin, Donald Manes, Andrew Stein, and Howard Golden. The "yes" votes were cast by Koch, Stanley Simon, and Anthony Gaeta.)

Just how morally objectionable Bellamy's decision against Charlotte Street was has become apparent with the passage of time. And with other votes Bellamy has subsequently cast in favor of luxury development projects that benefit the rich, like the Portman Hotel and the Lincoln West development on Manhattan's West Side. These three votes, analyzed together, suggest a planning vision of New York that would widen the gulf between the rich and the poor, and perpetuate the investment of disproportionate resources in Manhattan below Ninety-sixth Street at the expense of poorer neighborhoods in the outer boroughs.

The 2020-room, fifty-floor Portman Hotel, now going up at Forty-fifth Street and Broadway, is being built for rich tourists. It is being subsidized by the taxpayers with a $50 million loan from the state pension fund, municipal tax abatements and exemptions worth about $33 million, and a $21.5 million Urban Development Action grant from HUD. This should have been a totally private deal that either floated or failed on its own, in the free market of Reaganomics. There should never have been such lavish government underwriting for a project financially controlled by the Marriott Hotel Corporation, which owns nonunion motels and hotels all across the country.

On four separate occasions, Carol Bellamy and a majority of the Board of Estimate voted to approve funding, zoning, and land use aspects of the Portman deal.

Last September 16, Bellamy voted for another elitist project
—the $1 billion Lincoln West minicity for the rich on the West
Side. She voted for it even though every elected official from the
West Side was opposed to the project because of its oppressive
density, and because they felt a rail freight facility would make
better use of the same tract of land. But the project had the
support of the mayor Bellamy was supporting to become governor, of lawyer/fund-raisers John Zuccotti and Judah Gribetz, and
of all three daily newspapers.

On the day of the vote, a delegation of community leaders,
led by Bellamy's loyal friend Councilwoman Ruth Messinger,
visited Bellamy at 3 P.M. and pleaded with her to sponsor an
amendment reducing the density by 1000 units. For hours Bellamy was frozen in indecision—"an emotional basket case," according to someone who saw her. Bellamy kept the entire Board
of Estimate and City Hall press corps waiting until 1:30 A.M.
before she could make up her mind. And then she voted in favor
of the project, without ever trying to get consideration for the
community's compromise.

On March 22, 1983, State Supreme Court Justice Richard
Wallach invalidated the city's approval of Lincoln West and
mandated a new environmental study that would evaluate an
alternative project, half the density of the original. Wallach's
judicial action came in response to a lawsuit filed by a coalition
of West Side elected officials and community groups.

Political and intellectual independence is never easy to maintain. At some point in their careers, most reformist politicians
have to confront their own feelings of exhaustion, rejection, and
frustration. They all must face a series of small temptations and
compromise in order to become more legitimate to a broader
constituency. Or to become less threatening to some segment of
the establishment. Or to avoid ostracism inside their own legislative body. The need for acceptance is a universal human emotion.

But sometimes it is this hunger for approval—a need to please
everyone—that makes political leaders like Carol Bellamy (or
Hubert Humphrey, Bobby Wagner, or fill in the name) lose their
own identities. It is not so much selling out as giving up.

But some political leaders never give up. They never lose faith
in their own value systems. Often they become honored as vision-

aries or civic consciences late in their careers. But sometimes they also have a greater impact on legislation—and on their times— than the poll-taking pragmatists who fly with every fashion. Estes Kefauver surely left a greater mark on the Senate than Birch Bayh.

Locally, we have role models in politics who provide alternatives to the Bellamy model of ambition, confusion, and capitulation. We can see elected officials of endurance and fidelity becoming effective and raising consciousness—people like Robert Abrams, Ruth Messinger, Al Vann, Franz Leichter, Frank Barbaro, and Major Owens. They all possess an intellectual and psychological strength that has allowed them to sail against the wind, outlast fashions, and lately gain in credibility because events have vindicated their ideas. They have gained legitimacy by bending history toward themselves, rather than tilting themselves toward current events.

Koch was defeated for governor last year by a coalition led by unions and minorities; black voter registration and turn-out are increasing; the antinuke movement is growing; the J-51 tax-abatement program for landlords is slowly being reformed; the capital gains tax on property owners has been reinstated.

But somewhere along the way Carol Bellamy got lost. She lost the nerve to sail against the wind; she lost the inner confidence that history would eventually validate her ideas. She surrendered to the powerful temptation for immediate respectability and power. She altered her self-image to conform to the establishments' definitions of reality.

If studied as isolated events, Bellamy's decisive vote to kill the south Bronx housing project, or her campaigning for Koch, or her betrayals of political sisters like Virginia Apuzzo and Susan Alter, or her acceptance of a subminimum wage law might each be rationalized, or excused, or outweighed by other more humane and courageous actions.

But looked at together, over five years, all these separate, disappointing judgments develop a synergistic effect on each other. They make a pattern. They become the dominant trend of a political life. Sadly, they form a requiem for a reformer.

May 3, 1983

JOHN MURPHY: THE WORST CONGRESSMAN

John Murphy, Democrat of Staten Island and lower Manhattan is the most powerful member of New York City's congressional delegation. Murphy is the chairman of two committees that together give him authority over a budget of $1.3 million and a hundred jobs. Last year his seniority gave him control over all national Democratic Party campaign funds available to congressional candidates in New York.

And almost every variety of vice, almost every sample of sleaze, that might serve to illustrate the axiom "power corrupts" can be glimpsed in John Murphy's seventeen years in Congress.

- Murphy has misused his office to lobby for the recently evicted right-wing dictators of Iran and Nicaragua, helping to assure that millions of dollars in aid were exported to those foreign tyrants. Murphy has also engaged in a series of complex, private business deals involving the Shah of Iran and General Anastasio Somoza of Nicaragua that are now under criminal investigation by a federal grand jury.

- Murphy has consistently voted to favor privileged interests, especially the oil and shipping industries. He has sponsored legislation beneficial to these special interests but harmful to his own 470,000 constituents, and he has manipulated the machinery of government to perform favors for his campaign contributors—favors that provide no nourishment to his own district, now troubled with pollution, economic stasis, and shrinking municipal services.

- Murphy has improperly intervened with a federal regulatory agency to gain preferential treatment for a trucking company owned by Carlo Gambino's son.

- Murphy has been guilty of junketeering, absenteeism, payroll abuse, residency deception, and of distributing misleading campaign literature.

John Murphy is smart: he finished at the top of his graduating class at West Point and was class president. John Murphy is brave: he was wounded in Korea and was justly awarded the Purple Heart, Distinguished Service Cross, and the Bronze Star. John Murphy is tough: he has conquered every competitor for his congressional seat since 1962. Murphy had the potential to become the hero in politics that he was in war.

But John Murphy had too many distortions in his values, too many defects in his character. He has too much identification with the authoritarian personality; too much greed and selfishness; too much cynicism about human nature and the memory of voters.

Murphy declined, through his lawyer, to be interviewed for this article after I submitted a list of "general areas" I wanted to question him about. Murphy also refused to make public his 1978 federal tax return. Governor Carey, Mayor Koch, Comptroller Goldin, and Council President Bellamy have all made full public disclosure of their 1978 income tax returns.

Murphy has also declined to be interviewed for articles written about him by Ann Crittenden that were published in *The New York Times* on January 20, 1979, and October 26, 1977.

I spent nine months preparing and researching this article and interviewed more than a hundred people. Murphy's ideology is neither the subject nor the cause of this inquiry. He may well be the most conservative member of New York's congressional delegation, but that is not my primary concern here.

There are many honorable and scrupulous conservatives holding elected office in New York. Councilman Peter Vallone, Assemblyman Dominick DiCarlo, and State Senator John Marchi come to mind. One can differ with their ideas while still respecting their integrity. But Murphy is a special case because of his extraordinary pattern of conflict of interest, abuse of power, and of using his influence on behalf of those who pay for it.

In 1975, John Murphy had the worst attendance record of any elected representative from New York, New Jersey, or Connecticut. In 1977, Murphy was present for only 76 percent of roll call votes, the lowest attendance record in the New York City delegation except for Ed Koch and Herman Badillo, who were busy running for mayor. On June 8, 1978, Murphy was the only New

York City congressman who was absent when the full House voted on $2 billion in fiscal relief for New York City; Murphy was absent because he was in Athens, Greece, being paid $2000 by *Seatrade* magazine to give a speech. Murphy also received a $1300 airline ticket and $1650 in hotel expenses from the shipping publication. Murphy says he can't remember whether these payments were for his wife and son, but he acknowledges that they did accompany him to Athens, while New York's fate was being decided in Washington.

In 1978, Murphy received $108,000 in special interest campaign contributions, the third highest among all committee chairmen in the congress. In 1978, up until election day, out of 247 contributors who gave more than $100 to Murphy's campaign, only three were from Staten Island. And in July of 1978, Murphy was one of only four congressmen from New York who voted against even considering legislation to institute spending limits and public subsidies for political campaigns. This campaign finance reform effort was defeated, 213 to 196.

Murphy is the only New York congressman who keeps his county leader on his own payroll, in an apparent no-show job. The public pays Jim Smith, the Democratic leader of Staten Island, $25,000 a year. But Smith does not work out of Murphy's congressional office; he conducts his politics and patronage work out of Democratic party county headquarters, where reporters can almost always find him. Mike Azzara did a story on this dubious practice in the May 28, 1978, Staten Island *Advance*. Murphy told Azzara that Smith was his "administrative assistant." Smith said he was a "community representative."

Murphy is the only member of the New York delegation who, in 1978, accepted the absolute legal limit of outside speaking fees —$25,000. On September 20 of that year Murphy voted in favor of repealing the limit on earned outside income for members of Congress. However, this amendment to permit congressmen to earn unlimited incomes above their government salaries of $57,000 was defeated, 290 to 97.

Murphy claims as his legal voting address 150 Mada Avenue on Staten Island. But that is the home of his parents. Although it may be a legal residence, Murphy does not really live in his district. He owns a $130,000 house at 4810 Scarsdale Road, in

Sumner, Maryland. And last year he bought and sold a home in Longport, New Jersey, making a $68,000 profit on the transaction. But he calls those who run against him "carpetbaggers."

In 1975, Murphy took more junkets than any other member of Congress, making five overseas trips at taxpayer expense. In June of 1979 Murphy was publicly rebuked by White House staff members for going on a six-day junket to the Paris air show and missing key committee votes on legislation he was sponsoring.

"There are legitimate trips abroad and the Paris air show is not one of them," said Fred Wertheimer of Common Cause.

"It's a traditional junket, no matter how you describe it," said Russell Hemenway, national director of the Committee for an Effective Congress.

On June 15, 1977, the *Wall Street Journal* reported on how Murphy successfully deleted from a bill a provision that would have given the Federal Power Commission new powers to investigate anticompetitive practices among utilities and to issue orders prohibiting any unfair methods of competition.

The following year, in 1978, Con Edison contributed $500 to Murphy, more than the utility gave to any of the other seventeen congressmen from New York.

In the entire oil-consuming, inflation-squeezed Northeast, Murphy is the only congressman who consistently votes the way the oil companies would like him to vote. Murphy acts like he was elected from an oil-exporting state like Texas.

On May 2 of this year, the House Commerce Committee defeated by a vote of 22 to 21 a resolution to reject President Carter's damaging policy of oil price decontrol. The deciding vote in favor of decontrol was cast by Murphy. Every other congressman from the Northeast voted against this oil industry rip-off, including Republicans Matthew Rinaldo of New Jersey and Mark Marks of Pennsylvania. Murphy also voted in favor of deregulation of natural gas, which means higher profits for energy corporations and higher prices for consumers.

On June 28 of 1979, the full Congress voted on the crucial Jones-Moore amendment. This amendment would allow the oil industry to keep about *$6 billion* more in profits by reducing the windfall profits tax on oil companies by 10 percent below the formula drafted by the House Ways and Means Committee. It would also abolish most of the windfall profits tax by 1990. The oil industry flew dozens of lobbyists to Washington in Lear jets to promote the amendment. It was passed, 236 to 183. John Murphy was the only Democrat from New York City to vote for it. Leo Zeferetti, Mario Biaggi, Geraldine Ferraro, James Scheuer, and other more conservative members of the city delegation all voted in the interests of their consumer-constituents. Moreover, Murphy switched his vote to "yes" after the roll call was completed.

Among Murphy's other special-interest donations in 1978 was $1650 from members of the American Tuna Boat Association in San Diego. Murphy also received a $2000 honorarium and a free trip to San Diego from the U.S. Tuna Foundation on March 15, 1978.

In return, Murphy has tried to increase the number of porpoises that tuna fisherman can legally kill, the main goal of the tuna fleets. In 1977, Murphy bypassed his own committee's subcommittee on wildlife and conservation, which had a proenvironmental majority, to introduce legislation that would have increased the annual kill quota for porpoises from 59,050 to 78,900. The Murphy bill would also allow the killing of 6500 eastern spinner dolphins each year, even though this species has been declared "depleted." On May 13, 1977, the *Times* published an editorial attacking Murphy's porpoise-killing bill.

Nevertheless, Murphy's 1978 campaign literature boasted that he helped "protect such threatened mammals as whales, seals, porpoises, dolphins, walruses, and polar bears."

Murray Kempton once wrote that John Murphy "is more susceptible to the attractions of foreign tyrants than Oscar Wilde ever was to bellboys."

I will soon describe Murphy's extraordinary entanglements with the sadistic Shah of Iran. But let us begin with a summary of Murphy's many favors for General Anastasio Somoza of Nicaragua.

In 1976, Ed Koch was a congressman and the foremost human rights critic of Somoza's tyranny. Murphy, in an effort to mute Koch's criticism, arranged a lunch meeting for the three on May 30, 1976, at the Waldorf Astoria Hotel in Manhattan. Koch later described this meeting with Somoza and Murphy in an article he published in the August 8, 1977, edition of the *Voice*.

In May of 1977, Koch organized a successful campaign in the House Appropriations Committee to cut off $3.1 million in military aid to Somoza. Murphy led the counterattack on the floor of the House, which finally voted 225 to 180 on June 23, 1977, to restore all the weaponry to Somoza. Murphy and Somoza celebrated by spending July 4 together in Nicaragua. In May of 1978 the Carter administration released $12 million more in economic aid to Somoza as a result of pressure applied by Murphy and Representative Charles Wilson of Texas.

In October of 1977, a spokesman for Somoza admitted that Murphy had visited Somoza "at least a hundred times." Dr. Pedro Chammoro, the great journalist and editor who was later murdered by Somoza's gunmen, publicly called Murphy a "Somoza agent" when Chammoro was honored by Columbia University on November 1, 1977. He noted that Murphy stayed in one of Somoza's homes when he visited Nicaragua, and that he used Somoza's airline to get there.

As Somoza's corrupt and barbaric regime began to unravel, Murphy became almost a full-time agent of this foreign power. In September and again in November of 1978, Murphy flew to Nicaragua to hold press conferences with Somoza, attacking the insurgents as communists.

On June 20, 1979, ABC-TV reporter Bill Stewart was executed in cold blood by Somoza's guardsmen while covering the last days of the civil war. Murphy, incredibly, told the Staten Island *Advance* that "Stewart shouldn't have been there." He even went so far as to imply in an interview with the Staten Island *Register*, that the tape of the killing, which was shown on all three network news programs, was somehow a misleading distortion.

"What did you really see?" Murphy asked the *Register*'s Brian Haugh. "All you saw is what the camera showed you."

Stewart was killed with an American-manufactured weapon, a weapon possibly supplied as a result of the 1977 $3.1 million aid authorization bill that Murphy led the fight to approve.

The last week of June, the United States ambassador to Nicaragua—Lawrence Pezzullo—went to Somoza's bunker for a sensitive meeting where the ambassador planned to ask for the dictator's resignation and exile. Pezzullo was shocked to discover

Murphy sitting on Somoza's side of the negotiating table. He had no advance knowledge that Murphy would be at the meeting— *as an adviser to Somoza!* Murphy was invited to the meeting by Somoza, not by the American government, and he got there on a Nicaraguan military plane.

Murphy's journey to Somoza's side was made in secret and was not announced by his office. Even his own staff didn't know where he was. The *Washington Post* first disclosed the meeting on June 30. Murphy admitted to *Post* reporter John Goshko that he flew to Nicaragua with Somoza's foreign minister Julio Quintana, and that "I did not go as a representative of the U.S. Government." Before the *Post* blew Murphy's cover, his aides told reporters that he was "away on personal business."

The July 2 Staten Island *Advance* published an editorial admonishing Murphy for his diplomatic meddling, and pointing out that by going Murphy had "missed an important committee meeting at which Mayor Koch requested an extension of the 1981 deadline for the end to ocean dumping of sewer sludge. That issue is of some concern to Mr. Murphy's constituents since the city has proposed that Staten Island be made the dumping ground for dried sewer sludge. . . . Those who voted to send Mr. Murphy to Congress have a right to know why their interests have been placed second—even briefly—to the interests of Mr. Somoza."

A few years ago, Murphy accused Jane Fonda of treason for visiting Hanoi during the Vietnam war. But Murphy's own dictator diplomacy on behalf of a foreign head of state, conducted in secret and in conflict with the president's foreign policy, seems to me of greater concern to a grand jury than anything Fonda ever did.

Also last June, Murphy wrote a letter to President Carter saying that "several hundred Cuban troops are now in Costa Rica" and claiming that the State Department disputed Murphy's allegation, stating publicly there was no proof or evidence to back up Murphy's charge.

On August 1, 1979, Murphy accused the new Sandinista government in Nicaragua of the systematic executions of 3000 people. The American State Department publicly denied Murphy's claim, saying that it "flies in the face of all we have heard from there."

One of Murphy's errands for Somoza is now under investigation by the Justice Department. During the Arab oil embargo of 1973–1974, Murphy attempted to arrange Iranian financing and allocation of Iranian crude oil for a refinery then being planned by Somoza at Monkey Point. The Somoza regime was in desperate need of oil at that time.

On July 3, 1973, Murphy wrote a letter on his congressional stationery to the chairman of the National Iranian Oil Company, recommending that Iran participate in the refinery project and in a tanker company that was to be created as part of the deal.

Murphy closed his letter by writing: "During the visit of the Shah to the United States later this month, I would be happy to arrange a convenient meeting with General Somoza to clarify any of our previous submissions."

The company in Nicaragua that would have operated the refinery was 96 percent owned by General Somoza. The deal eventually fell through, but the question remains: Why would a United States congressman try to broker an oil deal between two foreign dictators?

Another avenue of the wide-ranging criminal investigation is Murphy's role with Burmah Oil Tankers and its former president Elias Kulukundis. Kulukundis himself is under investigation by a federal grand jury for siphoning funds out of his own company and back-dating documents. In the late 1950s Kulukundis was indicted and acquitted on charges of conspiracy to defraud, and for filing a false statement in the purchasing of government ships.

Murphy admits that he made representations to his friends in high places in Iran to provide a source of Iranian crude oil for Burmah Oil, which wanted to build a refinery in the Bahamas and later at three other locations. Murphy's intervention for Burmah Oil occurred in late 1973 and 1974, during the Arab oil embargo.

Murphy and Kulukundis are close friends, and Kulukundis has been a contributor to Murphy campaigns. In 1973, Murphy wrote a letter to Iranian officials, on congressional stationery, proposing they help out Kulukundis with allocations of crude oil, then a precious and scarce commodity.

Later in 1973, Murphy traveled to Tehran, where he personally conferred with Iranian officials about the proposed refinery in the Bahamas. In March of 1974, Murphy wrote a letter to Parvis

Mina, a director of the National Iranian Oil Company, requesting a letter acknowledging their prior meeting, and asking that more information be sent to Burmah Oil about the proposed refinery.

During the first six months of 1974, Murphy made two more trips to Tehran, both at his own expense, he says.

On April 11, 1974, Kulukundis wrote to Murphy that Burmah Oil Tankers is "preparing the appropriate economic, marketing, area, transportation, cost, and profit studies. . . . Together with you, we expect to personally present these studies in Iran during the early part of May." Kulukundis also wrote to Shariff Emani, of the Pahlevi Foundation in Tehran, offering to make a grant of $90 million to the foundation if the refinery deal was made.

Copies of other documents obtained from Burmah Oil indicate that Murphy was also an intermediary between the oil company and high Iranian officials for another Burmah Oil refinery being planned in Maine, for which the National Iranian Oil Company would supply crude oil "on a most favored customer basis and price" for twenty years.

On March 4, 1974, the vice-president of Burmah Oil Tankers sent Murphy "the most recent study of our 250,000 B/d [barrels per day] refinery project in Sanford, Maine, for confidential use in your preliminary discussions" in Iran.

Another document obtained by the *Voice* is a copy of a legal agreement between Burmah Oil Tankers and Murphy regarding negotiations for a refinery to be built along the Caribbean coast of Nicaragua, which Burmah Oil would operate, and for which the National Iranian Oil Company would supply crude oil. The negotiations failed, but the draft contract between Burmah's files (which may never have been executed) shows that Murphy was not doing charity and expected a great sum of money for his role as go-between.

The document provided that, if the negotiations were successful and an agreement consummated, "Burmah Oil shall pay to Murphy two-and-one-half percent of the gross cost of the entire project." This payment could not have been a legal fee because Murphy is not a lawyer.

The agreement draft also stated: "Burmah, as operator of the completed refinery, shall pay to Murphy the sum of five cents per barrel. . . . Payment to Murphy shall be made monthly in U.S.

dollars and the books and records of Burmah shall be available for inspection by Murphy or his authorized agents.

"It is understood and agreed that Murphy is involved with other negotiations directly or indirectly related to the aforesaid project [e.g., the obtaining of the oil, the financing and construction of the facilities] and by reason thereof, Murphy may receive compensation from Mundial or other parties, in addition to that provided for herein, and his receipt of such compensation shall not be deemed in conflict with the provisions hereof."

Recently, an audit of Burmah Oil Tankers' books and records was conducted by the highly respected accounting firm of Ernst and Ernst. The partner who performed the audit discovered $50,000 missing that could not be accounted for. This partner has told federal prosecutors that Kulukundis told him that the missing $50,000 was paid to a New York City congressman after being laundered through a political slush fund in the Bahamas. Kulukundis would not take my calls to comment on this matter.

Murphy's attorney, Andrew Maloney, has been notified by the Justice Department that his client is the potential target of a grand jury investigation into Kulukundis and Burmah Oil Tankers.

Murphy, however, continues to maintain publicly that he is not aware of any federal investigation involving his activities.

Murphy is also under scrutiny because of his role as a director of the Pahlevi Foundation of New York, which was a branch of the same foundation that sheltered the Shah of Iran's personal wealth in Iran until his tenure of torture was ended this year.

In his scholarly book, *Iran: The Illusion of Power*, Robert Graham of the *Financial Times of London* wrote: "Behind a smokescreen of charity, the [Pahlevi] Foundation is used in three key ways to assist the regime: as a safe and institutionalized conduit for 'pensions'; as a means of exerting control or influence by investing in specific sectors of the economy; and as a source of funds for royal ventures."

Graham estimated the assets of the foundation to be between $2.8 and $3.2 billion. These included investments in banks and insurance companies, a 25 percent stake in the Krupp Steelworks in West Germany, an interest in the National Iranian Oil Company, and gambling casinos in Iran.

In 1973, the Shah set up the tax-exempt Pahlevi Foundation of New York and appointed John Murphy to be one of its directors, with the power to represent the foundation in business transactions. The foundation hired the powerhouse law firm of Rogers & Wells, which, along with Murphy, was somehow able to convince the IRS to grant the foundation tax-exempt status as a charitable educational institution. The foundation was supposed to award scholarships to needy Iranian students, but it seems to have been used as a cover for members of the Shah's secret police (SAVAK) to infiltrate Iranian student-exile groups in this country. No scholarships were ever given out.

The tax exemption allowed the foundation to purchase title to property at the 650 Fifth Avenue site. Officers of several major construction companies have told reporters and federal prosecutors that they were informed by Nasser Sayyah, an Iranian playboy and an agent of the foundation, that they would have to kick back 5 percent of the construction contract to him if they wanted to be considered for the job.

Murphy has admitted to *Times* reporter Ann Crittenden that he was involved in the direct negotiations over the construction contract. He acknowledged that he advised one company on how to submit its bid.

Murphy is also a close friend of Nasser Sayyah. They have frequently been seen at parties together and Sayyah has admitted giving Murphy expensive gifts. Sayyah holds 1900 shares of stock in the American Chemsol Company, of which Murphy is chairman and in which Murphy holds stock valued by him at more than $100,000. Sayyah bought his stock from Murphy.

The bids for the Pahlevi tower were opened in Tehran, and the winning bid of $21 million was submitted by the late William Kelly, the chairman of the Frank Briscoe Company of New Jersey.

Federal investigators have reportedly discovered that in May of 1975, in Tehran, Kelly gave Nasser Sayyah a $300,000 check after being awarded the contract. This has been confirmed by sources close to the Briscoe Company. The check was then cashed in a gambling casino in Iran by Sayyah, thus converting it to untraceable cash and, in effect, laundering the payoff.

Murphy's role, if any, in this overall transaction is under

investigation by federal prosecutors. Sayyah is currently under subpoena to testify before a federal grand jury in Manhattan.

Sayyah is also being sued for $4.5 million for breach of contract by James Reed, a former assistant secretary of the Treasury in the Kennedy administration. Reed's suit alleges he signed a contract with Sayyah in May of 1973 to act on behalf of the Pahlevi Foundation in its acquisition of the 650 Fifth Avenue site.

Reed arranged for the Rogers & Wells law firm to be retained by the foundation, and he introduced Sayyah to Murphy. Sayyah and Murphy then became friends, and abruptly excluded Reed from all subsequent meetings, negotiations, and fees.

Sources in the construction industry say that Reed advised them to bid honestly for the Pahlevi job, without making any reference to kickbacks.

The cargo preference bill (HR 1037) made John Murphy famous. It was Murphy's impatient thrust into the upper reaches of national money and power. Murphy went to work drafting this bill as soon as he became the chairman of the Merchant Marine and Fisheries Committee in January of 1977. He rushed the bill through his own committee, which approved it 31 to 5, and he was the floor manager of the bill in the autumn of 1977; it became one of the most controversial issues of the session when millions of dollars were spent in a fierce lobbying campaign to pass it into law.

The cargo preference bill was an open and notorious piece of special-interest legislation worth many millions of dollars to a few shipbuilders, ship operators, and maritime unions. The bill would require that, by 1980, 9.5 percent of all oil imports—more than twice the current ratio—be shipped in tankers that are American-built and American-owned. The General Accounting Office did a study that concluded that this bill would cost consumers $240 million a year in higher prices for gas and home heating fuel. The reason for this is that American-flag tankers charge absurdly higher freight rates than all other foreign tankers, and the needless protectionism of the cargo bill would inflate prices along the line up to the individual consumer.

The *Wall Street Journal* of August 4, 1977, published an editorial called "The Maritime Payoff." It said: " 'Cargo Prefer-

ence' is a euphemism for a shipbuilder and maritime hijacking of
American consumers. East Coast consumers, who depend heavily
on imported oil, will be among the hardest hit. Constituents of
Merchant Marine Committee Chairman John Murphy can expect to pay an added $50 a year just for this bit of special-interest
legislation."

The New York Times, in an August 6, 1977, editorial, called
the cargo preference bill "a new way for ship owners and the
maritime unions to get rich at public expense. . . . It would violate
United States treaty obligations. And it would cost consumers
between $200 and $800 million per year in higher oil prices."

The *Times* editorial also pointed out how the shipping industry already received considerable underwriting and welfare from
the federal government—$236 million in subsidies for ship con-
struction and another $388 million in ship-operating subsidies.

But big power and big money were behind Murphy and his
cargo quota bill. Among the paid lobbyists working for the bill
were three former congressmen—Wendell Wyatt, an Oregon
Republican, and Democrats Ed Edmondson and James O'Hara.
Others hired to apply pressure for the bill included top Washington lobbyist Thomas Boggs, experienced Democratic party organizer Bob Keefe, and Charles McBride, the former director of the
Senate Democratic Campaign Committee.

An ad hoc committee of the bill's industry supporters retained
Gerald Rafshoon, the president's imagist, to run an advertising
campaign on behalf of the bill. The budget for this campaign was
$1.2 million. The media blitz included slick and effective full-page
ads in the *Times, Washington Post, Los Angeles Times,* and forty
other newspapers including the *Voice,* double-page displays in
the news magazines, and television commercials in fourteen cities. After the hiring of Rafshoon, President Carter gave the cargo
bill his personal backing. And a few months later, Rafshoon's
Atlanta advertising agency received a $125,000 contract from the
National Maritime Council.

The maritime unions also spread their money around. According to an analysis prepared by Common Cause, maritime interests
donated $448,000 to 215 congressmen elected in 1976; $82,000
to twenty-four members of Murphy's committee, including
$16,200 directly to Murphy; and another $9950 to Murphy in

June of 1977, while the bill was being debated inside Murphy's committee and during a nonelection year.

Maritime interests also contributed $50,000 to Murphy's 1978 reelection campaign, and on June 12, 1979, they kicked in $16,000 at a Washington cocktail party for his 1980 election. Moreover, Murphy collected $11,500 in speaking fees from the maritime industry and its unions during 1978.

President Carter got $200,000 in contributions from the maritime lobby during his 1976 campaign.

Albert Hunt wrote a story for the *Wall Street Journal* (September 30, 1977) that quoted Ben Man, the lobbyist for a maritime union, telling first-term Democratic Congressman Peter Kostmayer: "You'll recall when we gave you the $500 check last year, you gave us a pledge to vote for this bill." Representative Kostmayer told the *Journal* that he never made such a pledge and that he intended to vote against the cargo bill.

With Carter, Rafshoon, big-name lobbyists, and more than $2 million on his side, Murphy was confident his bill would become law and he would become a national power broker. On August 2, 1977, after Murphy's committee voted 31 to 5 in favor of the bill, Murphy put out a press release calling the committee vote "one of the most significant events in America's history as a maritime power."

The push for the cargo bill was too much like Murphy himself. It was overkill; it was too brazen, too greedy. It was being done too fast, and with too much money. It began to foment a backlash.

The *Times, Washington Post,* and *Wall Street Journal* all published editorials against the bill within a week after Murphy's committee reported it out. The *Post* wrote: "As national policy, it's got absolutely nothing going for it." On August 17, Fred Wertheimer of Common Cause released the analysis of shipping contributions and said: "The maritime industry and the cargo preference bill represent a textbook example for those who wonder how special-interest campaign financing is used to influence government decisions."

Typically, Murphy chose to rebut his critics with a harsh, personalized attack that was lacking in thought and substance. He accused Common Cause of "doing the out-front bidding of the oil industry." And he charged that the editorials in the *Times* and *Washington Post* were motivated by the revenue the papers received from advertisements purchased by oil companies. This is the same Murphy who complains whenever any reporter even suggests that his own votes might be influenced by his campaign financing. The *Wall Street Journal,* Murphy said, was "part of a profit-making conglomerate. We understand their taking special-interest positions."

The full House of Representatives voted on the cargo bill on October 19, 1977. In a chaotic scene, the House voted first by a voice vote. Without individual responsibility, the Murphy bill was passed overwhelmingly. Then Representative Paul McCloskey, the ranking Republican on Murphy's committee and an opponent of the bill, asked for unanimous consent for a roll call vote that would record each representative individually.

Murphy rose to object to the roll call. But his friend, conservative Republican Robert Bauman of Maryland, urged Murphy to withdraw his objection because the issue was so controversial and because Murphy probably had the votes anyway.

The roll was called, and with accountability in the chamber, the Congress defeated the cargo preference bill, 257 to 165. More than half the congressmen switched their vote when they knew it was no longer an anonymous shouted "Aye."

In his fine book *Vicious Circles,* Jonathan Kwitney described Tommy Gambino as "the new kingpin" of the garment district. Gambino is not only the son of Carlo Gambino, the late Mafia boss, he is also the son-in-law of Thomas Luchese, who was also a man of respect in organized crime.

In November of 1972, the New York City Police Department publicly named six garment-district trucking firms as mob fronts that were monopolizing curb space. Tommy Gambino was an officer of three of those companies—Consolidated Carriers, Dynamic Delivery, and Greenberg's Express.

John Murphy has gone to extraordinary lengths between 1971 and 1975 to pull strings and use his influence for Tommy Gambino, years that Gambino's father was the most powerful gangster in America, years during which Tommy Gambino's companies were receiving front-page publicity as Mafia-connected.

Tommy Gambino was not a constituent of John Murphy's. His trucking companies were not located in Murphy's congressional district. And all the favors Murphy did for Gambino he did himself. He never delegated them to a staff member.

Tommy Gambino needed the approval of the Interstate Commerce Commission to truck garments from Manhattan to Suffolk County. The ICC rejected Gambino's application as vice-president of Consolidated Carriers both on fitness grounds (his father) and on professional grounds; the company had neglected to comply with ICC rules and reporting requirements, including failure to list amounts of cargo and destinations.

So the Godfather's son took his problem to John Murphy. Murphy admits that in 1972 he met with Gambino and then called his good friend Robert Oswald. Oswald was then the $47,000-a-year congressional liaison officer for the ICC.

Murphy arranged for Gambino to meet Oswald, a man whom Murphy had already recommended be promoted to ICC commissioner. Murphy also asked Oswald to suggest the right lawyer for Gambino. Oswald, who is supposed to regulate trucking companies, ended up arranging a meeting between Gambino and Washington lawyer Theodore Polydorff, who then became Gambino's attorney before the ICC. Oswald later said he did this as a courtesy to Murphy.

Murphy also personally met with Oswald several times to argue that the ICC's enforcement division's ruling against Gambino should be overturned. Murphy says these meetings were just to make sure there was no discrimination against Gambino because of his father's name or reputation.

Murphy also admits to twice meeting with ICC Commissioner Robert Gresham to discuss Gambino's license application. One meeting was in Murphy's office and the other at the ICC.

John Murphy is an important person to the ICC, the way he was an important person to the Navy Department. Murphy has been a member of the House Committee on Interstate and Foreign Commerce for fifteen years. This committee has oversight authority over the ICC and a say in how big the ICC's budget is going to be. This committee handles all legislation the ICC might be concerned about. John Murphy is one of the most senior Democrats on this committee. So Commissioner Gresham had to take Murphy's personal interest in Gambino's license very seriously.

Soon after these meetings, the ICC reversed itself. Tommy

Gambino was given a license and expanded jurisdiction and was also given permission to take over another trucking company—Greenberg's Express.

Murphy has also acknowledged that he personally telephoned the New York City Police Department in April of 1973 to protest the police giving so many tickets to Gambino's trucks and listing his companies as fronts for organized crime.

Oswald was subsequently suspended and then fired by the ICC for conflicts of interest and for disclosing confidential information. Later Oswald was indicted for allegedly accepting $4000 in cash—bribes and two free trips—in exchange for giving Tommy Gambino his license.

At the trial, two witnesses—lobbyist Daryl Flemming and Gambino hoodlum Edward Lubrano—testified that Oswald had been bribed in the Gambino licensing reversal. But Oswald was acquitted by a jury.

Murphy was a witness during Oswald's trial. He admitted meeting with Tommy Gambino several times, starting in August of 1971, and having numerous phone conversations with Gambino. Murphy also testified that he personally called Gambino to inform him that the ICC had approved his license applications and that the ICC had given him advance notification of Gambino's approval.

On other occasions Murphy has described Gambino as "a boyhood" friend from their high school days at the La Salle Military Academy in Oakdale, Long Island. But at the trial Murphy said he was four years older than Gambino. Their overlap at La Salle could only have been a few months in 1943, when Murphy was a senior and Gambino a freshman.

Tommy Gambino's license from the ICC is worth about $150,000 a year in increased business to Consolidated Carriers.

Normally, if a resident in Murphy's district has a problem with a federal agency, if he is lucky a low-level staff person might be assigned to make an inquiry. But Murphy personally pressured the ICC for Gambino, personally helped get him a lawyer, personally met with ICC commissioners and staff members, personally helped persuade the ICC to change its administrative decision in the Gambino case, and personally was given the first call that Gambino would get his lucrative certificate.

The mystery is why Murphy would do all this for someone who was not even a constituent.

It is the commonplace disappointment of American politics that the candidates we vote for, in the hope that they will represent the commonweal, end up representing a special interest, usually the dominant economic interest in their home district.

So it is no real surprise that Senator Russell Long of Louisiana and Representative James Jones of Oklahoma fight for the oil industry rather than for the common good of the polity. It is not unexpected that the congressmen from North Carolina speak for the tobacco industry. It is not unexpected that the congressmen from Michigan usually reflect the auto industry's ideas about the Chrysler bail-out and air pollution controls. Delaware Senator Joe Beiden frequently echoes the point of view of the DuPont Corporation on antitrust and corporate tax matters.

What makes John Murphy unique is that he has sold parts of himself to so many different privileged interests—and foreign interests—that provide no nourishment or benefit to his own district.

Murphy has represented Somoza's interests against the national interests of his own country. He represented the Shah's interests against the interests of the taxpayers. He represented the interests of the Todd Shipyard Company against the interests of the United States government. He represented the interests of Tommy Gambino against the interests of law enforcement.

Murphy pushed the cargo preference bill even though it meant his own constituents would have to pay higher fuel bills. He voted for both oil and natural gas decontrol even though it meant higher energy prices for his own constituents. He represented the distant special interest of California's tuna industry against the public interest of nature and the environment.

Murphy has spent his time working on private business deals for foreign nationals like Nasser Sayyah and Elias Kulukundis while neglecting the needs of his own district.

In 1973, Murphy told a Ralph Nader study group: "I have no personal wealth."

Today, after six more years in Congress, he is a very rich man, with more than $100,000 worth of stock, an expensive home in Maryland, and a $68,000 profit on a home he sold in New Jersey.

And he refuses to make his tax returns public, even though many other elected officials have done so.

Nothing could better symbolize John Murphy's approach to public service than his own actions on June 8, 1978. While legislation to save New York City from bankruptcy with $2 billion in federal loan guarantees was being voted on by the United States Congress, John Murphy was in Greece getting paid $2000 to deliver a speech and getting free transportation and hotel accommodations worth $3000 for his family, all financed by a maritime industry publication.

John Murphy goes wherever the money is. John Murphy only does what enriches John Murphy. And to hell with his district, his city, and his country.

September 24, 1979

3

Civil Liberties
and Law Enforcement:
Balancing Rights

These are three articles that search for the appropriate balance between law enforcement and civil liberty, between protection from crime and protection of constitutional rights. These pieces explore the clash between equally valid and competing claims.

Maurice Nadjari is now a nearly forgotten name, but from 1972 to 1977 he commanded the attention of New York City as a special prosecutor, originally appointed by Nelson Rockefeller to clean up the criminal justice system. He had a vast budget, broad powers, and a large staff. He was frequently on television, and regularly on the front page of the *Times*. He was a force. But he struck me as a dangerous generic type—the prosecutorial zealot and overreacher. A Joe McCarthy. A J. Edgar Hoover. After covering a few trials, talking to other prosecutors, and studying a series of appellate opinions critical of Nadjari, I came to the conclusion that Nadjari was a bullying threat to constitutional protections. I then wrote an essay about him while he was running for district attorney in Queens in 1977. He lost the election, and he is now a defense lawyer whose name rarely gets into the papers.

In contrast, many critics accused ABSCAM of targeting, entrapment, and other prosecutorial excesses. But I found it to be a brilliant enterprise that caught seven corrupt lawmakers with creative, constitutional methods.

After trials and appeals in three separate federal jurisdictions, six congressmen and one senator were found guilty and were sentenced to prison. A 1,100 page report by a special Senate committee concluded that the rights of no individual defendants were violated, and that none of the congressmen was entrapped.

"Crime and the Certainty of Punishment" is a brief essay, written in 1976, that tries to force liberals and radicals to stop jerking their knees and think about predatory street crime in terms of common sense rather than rhetoric. I argue that swift trials and tougher sentences are necessary, and would not harm anyone's civil liberties. The piece antagonized some liberals, but as I suggested in the introduction to this book, I think growing up in the high-crime neighborhood of Brooklyn's Bedford Stuyvesant area cured me of any liberal guilt, and of any romantic illusions about the nature of street crime. I've always thought that poverty was a reason for crime, but never a justification.

IN DEFENSE OF ABSCAM

We must see the enactment and enforcement of stiff penalties for criminal behavior. The revolving door of criminal justice must be locked up tight. Those who choose to commit criminal acts must know that they will be responsible to the fullest extent of the law, and that restitution—where possible—is expected and that punishment is mandatory.

—JOHN MURPHY, February 3, 1980
political advertisement for himself

What follows is a meditation upon corruption. And an attempt to find an equilibrium between public integrity and civil liberty in the wake of ABSCAM.

Mistakenly, the question of leaks has received more notoriety from the ABSCAM operation than the issue of corruption. This emphasis has come from news executives and columnists who missed out on the leaks; from congressmen whose colleagues are on videotape taking money; and from defense lawyers who seem to be advertising for clients.

But as indictments come, and trials begin, I think the focus will shift to the more profound question of the systemic greed that has infected Congress, and most of politics. The leaks are unfair, and may do injury to due process. But they do not pose the same threat to democratic government as a pattern of secret corruption. The most fundamental lesson to be learned from ABSCAM may be the unimagined degree to which outright bribery influences public policy, legislation, and the realm of government favors, subsidies, licenses, franchises, approvals, and contracts.

Most of the congressmen implicated did not even propose a subterfuge of "legal graft" to the undercover FBI agents. They did not suggest that their payoffs be disguised as campaign contributions, legal fees, or speaking honoraria. Most of them are alleged to have stuffed the illicit cash right into their pockets.

If 8 out of 10, or 8 out of 20 congressmen who were offered cash accepted it, that is a remarkable ratio. Based on the ABSCAM sample, I would bet that the average unbonded Wall Street messenger is more trustworthy than the average congressman.

The ABSCAM sting is only the most recent shaft of sunlight to shine under the wormy rock of Congress. In the last five years, nine congressmen have been convicted of public corruption charges: Frank Brasco and Bert Podell of Brooklyn; Joshua Eilberg and Frank Clark of Pennsylvania; James Hastings of New York; Charles Diggs of Michigan; Andrew Hinshaw and Richard Hanna of California; Richard Tonry of Louisiana. Pennsylvania's Daniel Flood is awaiting trial for bribery and conspiracy. Buddy Leach of Louisiana is under indictment for vote buying. Three congressmen were "reprimanded" for failing to report Koreagate cash from Tongsun Park. Senator Herman Talmadge was "denounced" by the Senate for "reprehensible" conduct, including the diversion of campaign funds and office funds for his personal use. Moreover, credible law enforcement experts suspect that at least a dozen congressmen "got away with it" in Koreagate and will never be prosecuted for illegal payments accepted and concealed.

And two of the congressmen implicated in ABSCAM—John Murphy and John Jenrette—were already under investigation by the Justice Department for other possible federal crimes.

The corruption of Congress, and of politics in general, should be seen as part of a general climate of corporate influence and privileged access. Congress decontrols the price of crude oil and home heating fuel after taking campaign money from oil companies. Congress refuses to pass a hospital-cost containment bill after taking campaign money from the AMA. Congress votes millions of dollars in subsidies for shipping companies after accepting campaign money from maritime interests. Congress kills gun control legislation after accepting campaign money from the gun lobby. Congress increases the defense budget after accepting campaign money from defense contractors. That's the way it works, year after year.

There is a relationship between the gray area of conflicts of interest and legal graft, and criminal conduct itself. One can lead to the other. Once a public official has accepted a campaign contribution in return for a vote or favor, a line has been crossed and it is then easier to accept an unreported contribution and, finally, a bribe.

I do think the familiar litany of Ralph Nader/Common Cause reforms of campaign finance is valid and necessary. Public financing of campaigns, stricter financial disclosure, and regulation of lobbyists would improve the climate. But we must confront the crushing allegation that six congressmen have taken cash bribes that were never meant to be disclosed or reported, and would never be covered by any potential good government reform. I think that every member of Congress should be required to make his or her tax returns public. But I also think that the congressmen implicated in this scandal probably never intended to pay taxes on their payoffs. There is a limit to the value of the standard agenda of liberal reforms if public officials are going to behave like gangsters and take cash in suitcases and paper bags.

We have to think more deeply about the root causes of public corruption. I suspect one basic fault is the kind of people who are attracted to politics in the first place. Except for the handful like Elizabeth Holtzman and Ruth Messinger, who are motivated by idealistic values, the overwhelming majority are driven by an appetite for money, power, and status. Once in office, they will do anything to satisfy those appetites by financing campaigns and winning elections. Jimmy Carter will contrive a war hysteria. Jerry Brown will suddenly oppose gun control laws. Ed Koch will invoke the electric chair and polarize whites against blacks. Howard Baker will push for a useless, costly dam he knows will destroy the environment.

In the end, the common denominator among politicians becomes cynicism—"What's in it for me?" The Congress today is like the New York City Police Department in 1968. There is no peer group pressure to be honest.

Frank Serpico once told me that of the cops he graduated with from police academy, 10 percent were incorruptible, 10 percent were looking for ways to steal, and 80 percent would adjust to whatever the prevailing attitudes were. In narcotics enforcement, in Special Investigative Unit (SIU), the norm was to take, and almost everyone participated in the graft. That is certainly the situation described by Bob Leuci and Robert Daley in their book *The Prince of the City*.

I have the feeling that the moral atmosphere in the Congress today is not that different from what it was in SIU in the 1960s. The prevailing attitude seems to be that it's understandable to take some money for yourself. Crooks are not ostracized. During the two years of the FBI sting operation, not a single member of Congress reported an improper offer to a law enforcement agency. Congress does not have a few bad apples. The barrel itself is rotten.

The Congress has voted twice not to expel Representative Diggs, who has already been tried and convicted on felony corruption charges. Senator Talmadge was not stripped of his seniority, despite his fleecing the Senate of $40,000. The first time Senator Harrison Williams appeared on the Senate floor after the scandal broke, he was "greeted with handshakes and pats on the back," according to *The New York Times*. Even decent members like Ted Weiss reacted by demanding the FBI publicly apologize to Arabs throughout the world for perpetuating "an unjust stereotype" by having an undercover agent pose as an oil-rich sheik. That Ted Weiss would issue such a silly press release in order to be "one of the boys" illustrates the moral insensitivity of Congress.

When I say "one of the boys," I intend to suggest a macho element in the psychology of crooked politicians. It does appear to be a male club. Most women now in public office, like Holtzman and Messinger, do seem to have stronger values of integrity, although I don't understand all the reasons for this superiority. A woman lawyer friend of mine thinks that corrupt male pols are so sexist they wouldn't think of inviting a female colleague to share in a deal, even if she were willing. "Stealing among congressmen is a form of male bonding," she says.

The second root cause of public corruption is we, the people. Seven congressmen publicly charged with either criminal or unethical conduct in recent years have been reelected by their own constituents: Diggs, Flood, Fred Richmond of Brooklyn; George Hanen of Idaho; James Jones of Oklahoma; Ed Roybal and Charles Wilson of California. Two weeks ago, at P.S. 27 on Staten Island, I watched John Murphy receive a cheering ovation from 400 citizens of New York.

The bottom line is that the voting public has got to demand more honesty and excellence from their representatives.

Corruption is not a victimless crime. The victim—each time a public official violates his trust of office—is the principle of democratic government. And corruption is also a class issue; the poor can't afford to pay a bribe.

Without waiting to see the incriminating videotapes, and without access to any of the evidence, several pillars of the establishment have rushed into print charging that the ABSCAM case is based on entrapment.

Senator Adlai Stevenson III of Illinois, the former chairman of the Senate Ethics Committee, was the first to attack the concept of an undercover investigation that involved Congress. House Speaker Thomas "Tip" O'Neill concluded: "It was a setup, a goddam setup." Meg Greenfield denounced ABSCAM in her *Newsweek* column. And Alan Dershowitz was quoted by the *Times* as predicting: "We will probably not see successful prosecutions in most of these cases."

(For some reason Dershowitz is always identified as "a professor of criminal law at Harvard." In fact, he earns much of his income as an appellate lawyer for white collar criminals like Bernard Bergman, corrupt lawyers, pornographers, and dope dealers.)

Two days after the sting story broke, the *Washington Post* published an editorial that said: "No citizen—member of Congress or not—should be required to prove his integrity by resisting temptation."

This seems to be the crux of the matter. For years, law enforcement agencies have been employing undercover techniques to prove covert criminal conduct. For years, the courts and the press have applauded these innovative techniques. A few years ago, Brooklyn District Attorney Eugene Gold set up his own private carting company to expose organized crime's control of that industry in Brooklyn. Congressman Weiss did not demand that Gold apologize to all Italians.

Also, it is not as if these congressmen were unfairly tempted with offers of $1 million. A bribe of $50,000, in this era of uncontrollable inflation, is a modest payoff consistent with the free market.

The FBI has used the undercover sting method to indict and convict drug dealers, gun dealers, hijackers, counterfeiters, arsonists, and just two weeks ago, to arrest fifty of the nation's biggest pornographers. I do not believe that politicians should have any special immunity from the laws and court decisions that govern organized criminal activities in other institutions.

The *Washington Post* was dangerously wrong when it argued that a congressman should not be "required to prove his integrity by resisting temptation." Congressmen make our laws. Many will be tempted by bribery during their tenure in Washington. The public has a right to know if their representatives have the integrity to resist that temptation. White collar crimes like bribery are hard to prove. There is usually a satisfied buyer and a satisfied seller, no witnesses, and a secret, sophisticated transaction. It is not like a bank robbery where an alarm is set off and the investigation can begin immediately. Sometimes months go by before anyone becomes aware that a law has been broken. By then, it is often too late to prove what happened.

In New York City, we have a long list of suspected scandals without any criminal prosecutions: the $100 million cost overrun on the Yankee Stadium renovation; the direct lease day care

centers; Donald Trump's questionable real estate deals with the
MTA and UDC; the no-bid ninety-nine-year lease of the Bronx
Terminal Market to a campaign contributor; the millions "missing" from Ramon Velez's antipoverty programs; and the manipu-
lations surrounding the city's bus shelter franchise.

Without the proof of intent provided by audiotape or videotape, prosecutions are almost impossible in these circumstances.
That's why the undercover tool is necessary in the area of public
corruption, so long as it is done with strict court supervision and
monitoring.

Ever since *Sorell* v. *United States* in 1932, the Supreme Court
has been narrowing the definition of entrapment. The basic legal
test is now whether the suspect was "predisposed to commit the
crime." The Supreme Court has expressly approved the use of
"artifice and stratagem" to catch criminals. Chief Justice Charles
Evans Hughes, speaking for the majority, observed that government agents may properly "afford opportunities or facilities for
the commission of the offense."

In ABSCAM, it appears that each congressman implicated
was brought into the operation by a middleman or fixer serving
as a scout for corrupt opportunities. Congressmen were not
"tested at random," as some critics have claimed. Some greedy
congressmen heard about the bribe-giving from colleagues and
asked to be introduced.

Congressman Kelly, who stuffed $25,000 into his pockets and
asked, "Does it show?" was accompanied to the FBI's rented
townhouse by a Long Island Mafia hoodlum. Lawyers and businessmen served as facilitators, intermediaries, and bagmen for the
others.

Moreover, these public officials voluntarily went to yachts,
motel and hotel suites, and to the expensively appointed Washington townhouse, unaccompanied by legitimate staff, to meet
with shadowy people, and do business. I don't think honest politicians, or politicians taking their first bribe, would act that way.

ABSCAM began as an ordinary undercover investigation into
stolen art. It evolved organically to cover mobsters and public
officials in New Jersey, and then in the direction of Congress. If
Attorney General Civiletti or FBI director Webster had aborted
ABSCAM at the point the bagmen first boasted they had several

congressmen in their pockets, it would have been obstruction of justice and Congress would now be investigating a cover-up. They had a legal and moral obligation to investigate allegations against some of the most powerful men in Washington, most of them members of the president's political party.

Deputy Attorney General Philip Heymann has told the Congress that at one point early in the undercover phase "dishonest brokers offered, for a commission, to bring in federal, state, and local officials, who, in return for payments, would produce favors.

"We didn't say, 'No, we don't want that, we're only interested in stolen art.' "

Heymann testified that if the "dishonest brokers" had promised to bring President Carter to the townhouse, "I would have swallowed twice, but I wouldn't have stepped back."

As for monitoring the clandestine meetings with legally approved video cameras, that seems to me the best prevention against entrapment. Brokers and fixers, once captured, might fabricate allegations against public officials they didn't like in order to gain leniency or immunity. The videotapes are protection against a frame-up. Whatever occurred in those meetings is preserved on tape and will be played at public trials.

If any innocent congressman said: "How dare you offer me a bribe, I will report you to the police," we will soon know about it.

The great irony of ABSCAM is that the FBI—apart from its role in the leaks—has finally done something it can rightly be proud of. And now it is being criticized by the same people who used to criticize them for ignoring white collar crimes.

The fact is that there is a new, modernized FBI. J. Edgar Hoover ran the FBI for forty-eight years and during that period was responsible for more lawlessness than John Dillinger. During Hoover's dictatorial reign, Martin Luther King was the victim of illegal eavesdropping and character assassination; citizens were spied on and their homes broken into without warrants; the four Klansmen responsible for the bombing deaths of four black girls in Alabama were protected from prosecution; and public figures like Jean Seberg were tormented because of their political beliefs. Hoover resented Robert Kennedy's efforts to make organized crime a high priority and made the FBI concentrate on building up statistics by stressing relatively easy-to-solve crimes like auto theft. He had a Burger King concept of law enforcement—fast service of junk cases—to get bigger budgets.

As a result of Hoover's death in 1972, and the new FBI requirement of mandatory retirement at fifty-five, there has been a dramatic turnover. Today there are more than six hundred black and female agents; more than eight hundred accountants to solve complex white collar crimes; and a new, impressive leadership, including Director William Webster, and Neil Welch, who runs the FBI's New York office. In a world of limited resources, Welch helped provide the money and manpower to keep ABSCAM going. Twenty years ago, an undercover investigation like this would have probably ended with Hoover confiscating the video-tapes and blackmailing the congressmen, instead of with a prosecutor presenting the evidence to a grand jury.

I find the attacks, mostly from liberals, on the FBI's role in ABSCAM to be unfair. The liberal critics, who all favor the presumption of innocence and due process, are prejudging the FBI's tactics without waiting to learn any of the facts. It is as if Hoover were still FBI director, John Mitchell were still attorney general, and J. Wallace La Prade, who was fired in disgrace, were still in charge of the FBI's New York office. The critics seem to be quarreling with ghosts.

The officials who monitored ABSCAM most closely—Attorney General Civiletti, Deputy Attorney General Heymann, and FBI Director Webster—are all honorable, prudent lawyers.

The twilight nexus of organized crime, greedy public officials, and crooked businessmen is the most worthy subject of all for government inquiry. After a generation of abuse and excess in other areas, the FBI has finally plunged into this sensitive and risky realm. The FBI made the racketeering case against Anthony Scotto, and has cracked a nationwide horse-race-fixing racket. The Brilab sting in Louisiana may have caught the governor, two candidates for governor, and Carlos Marcello, the closest thing there is to a real Godfather. The FBI Miporn sting should be cheered. And so should ABSCAM, for the courage to apply the same standard of law and justice to the powerful as the powerless.

Last week a wise FBI agent, who works on corruption cases, said to me: "You know, if we could somehow stop all the payoffs

in this country to politicians, labor leaders, and corporate executives, I think we will have found the cure to inflation."
March 3, 1980

CRIME AND THE CERTAINTY OF PUNISHMENT

Crime is the most difficult public issue for liberals and radicals to think lucidly about. For me it is the only issue where what I think I am supposed to think conflicts with my experience, my instinct, and my common sense.

During the 1960s, I was uncomfortable with the radical rhetoric about crime. Having grown up in Bedford-Stuyvesant, I did not think muggers and purse snatchers were revolutionary guerrillas. I knew how terrible a problem violent street crime was for poor blacks. I did not think all cops were "pigs" to be shot in the back by "people's" heroes.

My inchoate thoughts about crime were compelled to become more focused in 1968, when I frequently debated on behalf of Robert Kennedy before audiences that were predominately sympathetic to Eugene McCarthy. Each time, middle-class and upper-middle-class liberals would vehemently attack Kennedy for stressing crime as a campaign issue in the presidential primaries. Kennedy, as a former attorney general, did feel strongly about both street crime and organized crime, and he campaigned as passionately against crime as he campaigned against the Vietnam war, hunger, or racism.

Many of the McCarthy activists, and McCarthy himself, argued that any reference to "law and order" was an appeal in code to racist voters, to the "Wallace constituency." These McCarthy backers usually lived in low-crime, expensive suburbs or in luxury apartment buildings with two doormen and elaborate surveillance systems.

I thought about their argument and decided I disagreed. Crime, to me, was a real issue. In fact, it was a *class* issue: Poor people were the victims. It was also a civil liberties issue. It is a constitutional right to move about free day or night, and this essential freedom was being eroded by the fear of crime.

A few years later, I got to know a cop—a good cop—who was a commander of a plainclothes unit in Bedford-Stuyvesant. Off and on, I would spend a night with him while he patrolled the streets. Unlike the rest of us, cops get to see the victims and survivors of crime. It can be traumatic to see the blood, and the tears, night after night.

My mother is in her seventies and has lived in the Bronx for fifteen years. She and her friends were—and are—terrified. There was a brutal murder in her building in 1975. There are old people in this city who subsist on the food neighborhood schoolchildren buy for them at the supermarket because they are so frightened of the elevator, the hallway, the dark street, that they do not leave their small apartments at all.

All during the past decade, liberals and radicals I know still tended to react in their own predictable fashion to crime as a public political issue. Some radicals advocated the abolition of all prisons. Liberals seemed biased against all prosecutors, whether the prosecutor was indifferent to civil liberties, like Maurice Nadjari, or whether he was committed to the Bill of Rights, like Joe Hynes. Liberals also tend to argue that the *only* remedy for crime is the abolition of poverty.

There is a proven relationship between unemployment and crime. But I also believe that one additional short-term solution to the epidemic of violent crime, especially by juveniles, is *certainty of punishment.* Law and order seems a positive objective for society. I am for it.

Law and order became a resonant code term for both bigots and common people, partly because "progressives" abdicated on the crime issue, reacting to the symbolism of the words and not to their literal meaning.

The evidence suggests that certainty of punishment may well be the most likely deterrent to violent crime. Not severity of punishment. Not capital punishment or Rockefeller's draconian drug law. Just swift trials and sure sentences. Today there is no certainty of punishment for the juvenile hunting gangs, sadistic predators upon the elderly. Most violent juveniles know that the first time, the second time, probably the third time they're arrested, they're likely to be quickly recycled by a family court judge back onto the street.

Most of these violent juveniles regard the criminal justice system as a game. They are cunning in all the ways to beat it. They know that witnesses become discouraged and memories fade as time passes, so they stall, make motions, and delay until their lawyers can maneuver the case before a lenient judge.

When I read *Thinking About Crime* by Harvard professor James Q. Wilson, I found myself agreeing with many of his points. Wilson argues that tougher sentences for repeated violent crimes might discourage the marginal criminal from predatory offenses. Wilson believes that some portion of the criminal population is rational and is not indifferent to the probable risks and rewards of the mugger's occupation. If the mathematical odds of going to jail are lowered, say, from 50 to 1 to 10 to 1, then some apprentice predators will think twice about their night's activity.

All the suggested remedies for the rising crime rate are problematic. No expert, no politician, no district attorney really knows what works, what actually will stop or reduce muggings, assaults, stick-ups, rapes—the crimes we all fear.

There is no evidence that the extreme conservative solutions have any merit—restoration of the death penalty, diminishment of the civil liberties made law by the Warren Court.

Some notions perceived as liberal are, I think, effective, particularly prison reform, drug treatment programs, stricter gun control laws, and the removal of licensing and employment barriers to ex-offenders.

But I am also convinced that if we made certain the prospect of swift, fair trials—say within four months of arrest—and then provided somewhat longer sentences for a second violent felony, that, too, would be effective in reducing crime.

For example, if I were sentencing an eighteen-year-old for

assault, and it was a second violent felony, I would sentence him to four or five years in prison. If it were a second attempted rape, I would give the defendant ten years without parole.

I would do this, knowing Attica and Clinton are as inhuman as Stalin's Gulag. I would do this, knowing there are no rehabilitation programs in those prisons. I would do it as a protection for the innocent, lawful citizens of this city. I would do it as a clear signal to other criminals that any other second offender who mugs or rapes or hurts someone will go to prison for a significant length of time.

I also think the pendulum has swung too far in the direction of protection of the rights of juvenile criminals. Last month, nineteen-year-old Ronald Timmons was arrested in the Bronx after he was caught robbing and severely beating an elderly woman. Timmons was released on $500 bail because the judge did not have legal access to the defendant's confidential juvenile criminal record. This juvenile record contained seventeen previous arrests, including a nonadjudicated accusation of homicide of a ninety-two-year-old man in 1972. The confidentiality of Timmons' juvenile-arrest record seems, on balance, less vital to the public interest than the judge's need to know it fully before making a decision to return someone like Timmons to his neighborhood. As it turned out, Timmons jumped bail and was captured last week in Baltimore.

Civil liberties groups and previous court decisions have sheltered juveniles who are arrested from being fingerprinted and photographed. But I am now persuaded that the rising crime rate and recidivism among violent juveniles make it in the public interest to both fingerprint and photograph these suspects. And if a fifteen-year-old is charged with murder, he should be tried and sentenced as an adult.

My reporting in the criminal justice system has convinced me that many sophisticated criminals employ juveniles to do their dirty work—torching a building, for example, or delivering heroin —because they know that even if they're caught, their cases will be treated lightly in family court.

I make these comments on crime and punishment because I think liberals and radicals have, in fact, ignored the reality of violent street crime. I think crime, and the fear of crime, is New

York City's tumor. It is scaring middle-class tax-paying families out of the city to the suburbs. This is eating away at the city's revenue base. Crime is literally killing the city.

In the long run, the causes of crime are, as ever, unemployment, racism, lack of education, and drug addiction. But poverty is only a reason for crime, not a justification.

The enormity of the crime problem requires those of us on the left to rethink our ideas about punishment with as much honesty, and as little sentimentality, as possible.

One fear I have is that the current hysteria about crime is setting the stage for some dangerous demagogue to run for mayor on a platform of round-ups of "undesirables."

Stricter, swifter, criminal penalties, especially against the juvenile hunting gangs, is a distasteful, simplistic remedy whose time has come.

December 6, 1976

NADJARI: IN HIS HEART HE KNOWS YOU'RE GUILTY

When Maurice Nadjari was sworn in as special prosecutor in September of 1972, he had the goodwill of the entire city behind him. His mission was noble and necessary. He was described— and perceived—as a hero, as a lone warrior against a corrupt system.

In four years Nadjari spent $14 million of the taxpayers' money. He indicted eleven judges but did not convict one of them. He never proved in a court of law that one senior public official took one dollar in graft. He obtained defective indictments with "inaccurate testimony" and "illegal wiretaps." He ruined careers with baseless charges. His office improperly leaked grand jury testimony to the media. He attacked the integrity of anyone who questioned his tactics. In the winter of 1976, the respected U.S. attorney David Trager said, "No prosecutor trusts or respects Nadjari, personally or professionally."

And Maurice Nadjari, with a staff of 175, and the most wiretaps in the city, lost every important case. Mackell, Cunningham, Levy, DeSapio, Goldman, the eleven judges—he lost them all.

Now, at the end of Nadjari's wild ride, two basic facts remain true and unchanged: there is still a lot of corruption within the judicial and political system, and despite Maurice Nadjari's dismal and dangerous record, he is still perceived as a lonely hero-warrior.

Nadjari has a built-in excuse. Every time one of his cases fails appellate scrutiny, he implies that the reversal or dismissal is only further proof that a corrupt establishment is conspiring against him. But Robert Morgenthau's cases against Carmine DeSapio and James Marcus led to convictions upheld on appeal. And David Trager's cases against Matty Troy and Nassau D.A. William Cahn led to convictions upheld on appeal. So did Joe Hynes' prosecutions of Bernard Bergman and Eugene Hollander. Only Nadjari's political cases lacked the competent legal work to survive the test of independent judgment.

Nadjari's original intentions were good. He was a competent prosecutor of simple crimes by cops and burglars. But his task in this job was to expose a subtle and sophisticated form of corruption. Some of his failures can be explained by the frustration caused by not accomplishing this difficult goal.

But the roots of Nadjari's excesses can be traced to his own personality and character. He seems to believe the end justifies the means. He sees the world in black and white, without doubts, without ambiguities. He is very ambitious, and this made him intensely concerned with personal publicity in a job in which he had no boss to hold him accountable.

He is obsessive and without a sense of proportion; in a frequently quoted speech, made to the National College of District Attorneys in 1971, Nadjari compared the thrill of a jury foreman saying "guilty" to the act of lovemaking.

Attorney Harvey Greenberg, who represented several clients

in face-to-face negotiations with Nadjari, told me: "In my opinion, Nadjari is mentally disturbed. He seems like a classic paranoid personality. His moods shifted wildly, like Captain Queeg. One minute he was rational, and the next he was acting like a maniac, making threats. . . . He treated me as if I were corrupt just for representing my clients, most of whom were never even indicted."

A judge has been quoted as saying that Nadjari "spontaneously alters events into an advocate's argument."

When I asked him why he preferred prosecution to defense work, Nadjari replied: "Because I know most defendants are guilty."

And, at the end, Nadjari became a complete fanatic, disregarding the rule of law and the Bill of Rights in a crusade to save his own job, which he equated with the office of special prosecutor, because by then he seemed to believe that he was the only honest man left in public life.

The lawyer who might have been the Seabury of this generation, the man who might have been another Archibald Cox, turned out to be another Joe McCarthy.

Now he is running for district attorney in Queens County as a Republican. He is eight points ahead in the polls, with only a 9 percent unfavorable rating and an 85 percent recognition factor.

The gap between the image and the reality, the discrepancy between Maurice Nadjari's reputation and his actual performance, is greater than that of any other politician in this city.

Maurice Nadjari's indictments were always front-page material and were usually reported as the first item on television news programs. We all remember the ritual arrivals of the sullen politicians in handcuffs to be booked and fingerprinted at the first precinct.

Months later, the appellate dismissals of these charges would be reported in the back of the papers and toward the end of the news shows. And, necessarily, without any memorable film footage. Recently, it took me the better part of a day to read the judicial opinions that threw out twenty of Nadjari's most publicized cases.

Four separate indictments brought by Nadjari against Bronx Democratic leader Patrick Cunningham were dismissed by Leonard Sandler, a judge who is revered for his integrity and balanced judgment. In throwing out the last indictment against Cunningham, Sandler wrote, in a forty-two-page decision, that the case was presented to the grand jury in a "shockingly improper and prejudicial manner," and that the prosecutor had sought "systematically to arouse prejudice against the defendant." (The prosecutor who presented the Cunningham case was Nadjari's chief assistant, Joseph Phillips.)

The indictment against sixty-five-year-old Judge Ludwig Glowa for having accepted a $500 bribe was thrown out for the complete lack of any corroborating evidence. This was done on a motion submitted by Nadjari's able successor as special prosecutor, John Keenan. Today Glowa is reported by his friends to be a shattered man and a recluse.

The appellate division reversed Nadjari's trial conviction of former Queens District Attorney Thomas Mackell. The unanimous verdict of the five appellate jurists stated that Nadjari was "guilty of constant and patent disregard of the basic rules of evidence." Nadjari tried this case himself.

The late justice John Murtagh dismissed Nadjari's perjury indictment of attorney, and former prosecutor, Alvin Geller. Murtagh's decision said Geller had been indicted solely on a "difference in the interpretation of words," and that Nadjari had presented "not a scintilla of evidence" to support his allegations.

Nadjari's indictment of Irving Goldman, the city's commissioner of cultural affairs, was dismissed by Justice Murtagh, whose decision stated Nadjari has been "wholly without authority" to bring it. Murtagh added that even presenting the case to the grand jury verged on "contempt" because he had already warned Nadjari the entire matter was outside his legal jurisdiction.

Nadjari's indictment of former City Tax Commission Chairman Norman Levy was dismissed by Justice Leon Polsky—another superb judge—because Nadjari had failed to bring the case to trial within six months, as required under the law.

In dismissing Nadjari's indictment against Judge Paul Rao, Sandler wrote an opinion saying, "Coupled with the fact that the evidence contains no intimation of any misconduct on his [Judge Rao's] part, I very much doubt that the grand jury would have voted the indictment if the evidence had been presented properly."

Nadjari's indictment against the late Justice Irving Saypol was dismissed because Nadjari had used illegal wiretaps.

Nadjari's indictment of Justice Jospeh Brut was dismissed because of many grand jury abuses, including "the introduction of a significant body of inadmissible hearsay testimony."

Justice Polsky dismissed Nadjari's indictment of Carmine DeSapio because of the lack of any corroborating witness and because of the use of insufficient evidence.

Justice Sandler threw out Nadjari's indictment of Judge-elect Anthony Mercorella. Sandler wrote that there was "not one word of evidence in the record that supports" Nadjari's contention that Mercorella had purchased his judgeship from Pat Cunningham.

And there were others. Fitzgerald. DiFalco. Kaming. Orlando. Sixty-three cases were thrown out. My day of reading produced a single inescapable conclusion: Maurice Nadjari had such contempt for the constitutional rights of grand jury witnesses that he could have indicted any citizen of this city if, in the closed chamber of his mind, he had decided this citizen was guilty.

Nadjari gradually lost the respect of his colleagues in law enforcement, of the defense bar, and of the appellate judiciary. The institutional base of his power—and the reason he remains so popular—is the media. One likely reason the media supported him was that Nadjari fed reporters leaks from the grand jury, leaks often so bereft of fact that they were nothing more than malicious gossip.

In June of 1973, *The New York Times* published a front-page story by Nicholas Gage under the headline: CITY GRAFT STUDY BEGUN BY NADJARI. The third paragraph of the story implied that Richard Lewisohn, the former finance administrator, was under investigation for placing city deposits in favored political banks. Three more stories appeared over the next four days, "linking" Lewisohn to the inquiry through "sources knowledgeable about the investigation."

Lewisohn is one of the most honorable men to serve this city in the last decade. He was never under investigation. But Nadjari never bothered to inform the press of that.

There were dozens of other innocent victims of this convenient collusion between a prosecutor desperate for publicity and journalists anxious for easy scoops and indifferent to civil liberties.

Marcia Chambers wrote a front-page story in the *Times*, stating that Bronx Civil Court Judges Herbert Shapiro and Bernard Herman were under investigation by Nadjari, "according to political and law enforcement sources." They were never indicted.

The *Times* ran a front-page story saying that former Deputy Mayor Richard Aurelio was under investigation by Nadjari for allegedly shaking down potential judges for contributions to John Lindsay's defunct presidential campaign. Nothing ever came of it. Nadjari never issued a statement that the investigation was closed. But Aurelio suffered personal financial losses and anguish to his family.

In March of 1974, Nadjari's attention turned to Brooklyn Supreme Court Justice Irwin Brownstein. Brownstein was a model judge. He had moved his courtroom into the Brooklyn House of Detention Christmas week of 1973 to hold hearings for hundreds of men awaiting trial, held in detention only because of bail they could not pay. He was the judge the Brooklyn D.A.'s office trusted with the most sensitive wiretap orders on organized-crime members. His reputation was for fairness, diligence, and compassion.

Then Nadjari's office began to leak: BROWNSTEIN NAMED AS THE JUDGE IN LAWYERS' ALLEGED BRIBE PLAN, said one *Times* headline. NADJARI WILL INSIST BROWNSTEIN WAIVE IMMUNITY ON TESTIMONY, said a front-page headline over a story by Nicholas Gage.

Nadjari's office let it be known that Brownstein was under subpoena to appear before a grand jury that was impaneled to investigate the sale of judgeships in Brooklyn. They let it be known that Brownstein's name was mentioned in a taped conversation involving the fixing of a case. And these stories appeared in the *Times*, which cited "sources close to the case" and "law-enforcement sources."

At the time, Nat Hentoff, Pete Hamill, and I wrote columns trying to remind people of Brownstein's superb record, of the constitutional presumption of innocence, and of the lack of any concrete proof of wrongdoing. But in a week of *Times* headlines a man's reputation can be smeared beyond defense or repair.

The following week Brownstein testified before the grand jury. The questions were all innocuous, and it was immediately clear that Nadjari had no justification for even questioning Brownstein. A year later, the grand jury's term expired, and Brownstein was never indicted.

Once, during a private dinner with Nadjari after the grand jury had been disbanded, I asked him why he didn't now make a public statement clearing Brownstein's name.

"What if I know in my heart that he is guilty?" Nadjari replied.

Recently I interviewed special prosecutor John Keenan about the Brownstein episode. Keenan, after reviewing the entire file, told me: "As far as I can tell, there is no evidence in our files that suggests that Brownstein purchased his judgeship."

I then asked Keenan about the alleged fixed case in which Brownstein's name was apparently used by a lawyer without his knowledge. Keenan said: "This office plans to ask Brownstein to be a people's witness in that particular case. I think you can fairly interpret that decision as exoneration or vindication."

Eighteen months after Brownstein's torment, the State Commission of Investigation released a 122-page report clearing him and concluding that Nadjari and his chief assistant, Joseph Phillips, had deliberately disclosed information to the press that "improperly tarnished" numerous public officials.

The report accused Nadjari of summoning Brownstein before the grand jury even though the special prosecutor's office knew that Brownstein "had nothing to do with the corrupt transaction" under investigation.

The report, which took seven months to prepare, also accused Nadjari of:

- admitting that he "probably" provided confidential information about a wiretap to Marcia Chambers of *The New York Times*

- having "lax or nonexistent administrative controls" in preventing leaks to the media

- allowing investigations to be "influenced by a concern for media favor"

- giving "contradictory and evasive testimony under oath" when the commission asked him about various leaks from his office

The report said that Nadjari's chief assistant, Joseph Phillips, was guilty of "improper disclosures and arrogant and roughshod disregard for the rights of others."

Brownstein was recently under consideration for an important law enforcement job in the Carter administration. The word came back through the grapevine that Brownstein wouldn't get it, because of the enduring stain placed on his reputation by Maurice Nadjari.

The reckless, ambitious, and paranoid part of Nadjari's personality took permanent command of him on December 23, 1975, when Governor Carey tried to remove him from the office of special prosecutor. In an effort to keep his power, Nadjari and his staff, over the next two weeks, said and leaked a series of irresponsible fictions that created a climate of near-hysteria.

On December 25, Nadjari said Carey's decision to fire him had been "triggered" by the "knowledge" Carey had about an investigation of Democrats close to Carey. No proof was offered. Nadjari also said he was "closer than I have ever been" to catching the hard-core political corruptors.

The next day Nadjari said: "Is the governor motivated by covering up corruption in firing me? Do we have our own Watergate?" No evidence was cited to back up this attack on the motives of the governor of the state.

Then came the Niagara of leaks. On December 31, the *Times*, in a front-page story by Marcia Chambers, reported that a wiretap had been placed in the office of Manhattan Surrogate Samuel DiFalco. This was not true; and it was unethical to leak, or publish, such a confidential fact even if it were true.

On January 6, Nadjari's office filed in open court a fourteen-page affidavit that seemed more yellow journalism than legal document. The affidavit accused Pat Cunningham, then Democratic state party chairman, of being "at the center of a corrupt marketplace of judgeships." The document, signed by Nadjari himself, went on to allege that Cunningham's "corrupt acts" were not limited to "selling judicial positions" but also accused him of taking bribes, and of being involved in the "improper handling of a case in the Bronx criminal court."

Such unsubstantiated allegations are almost never included in unsealed court documents, and of course none of these allegations was ever proven to be true in a court of law. They did, however, succeed in driving Cunningham out of his party office, and in building public support for Nadjari's rampage to retain power.

On January 8, Marcia Chambers wrote a page-one story that Bronx judges Bernard Herman and Herbert Shapiro were under investigation by Nadjari. They would never be indicted.

The same day, the *New York Post* published a huge front-page headline: DESAPIO BACK AS SECRET BOSS.

The lead of the story said that Nadjari had "uncovered evidence" that DeSapio "is once again the boss of the city's Democratic party."

In fact, all Nadjari had in his possession was one recorded conversation, during which one individual referred to DeSapio as "the chief." The whole notion was absurd. DeSapio was then sixty-seven years old and suffering from a bad heart. Nadjari's subsequent indictment of DeSapio, for one count of perjury, was swiftly thrown out for lack of evidence.

But all the sensationalism worked. Nadjari was given a six-month extension to continue in office. And every major indictment he brought during the six-month period was eventually found to be worthless. His lurid affidavit accusing Cunningham of taking bribes and fixing cases never had a basis in legal evidence.

A four-month investigation by the universally respected former judge, Jacob Grumet, found no facts to justify Nadjari's suggestion that Carey fired him to "cover up" his own "Watergate." Grumet's 101-page report concluded:

"There is no evidence to support the charge or allegation that the governor's decision to replace Mr. Nadjari was the result of any 'improper influences.' I also find that there is no evidence to support the allegation by Mr. Nadjari that an investigation pending in his office 'triggered' his proposed dismissal. . . . It is my firm belief that Governer Carey's decision to replace Mr. Nadjari was based upon his independent judgment."

Nadjari's response was to attack the integrity of Grumet's report.

A week after the publication of the report, Nadjari's six-month extension ended, was not renewed as he had hoped, and he left the office of special prosecutor. At his farewell press conference, on June 28, 1976, Nadjari uttered one last smear. He said that Attorney General Lefkowitz, who had appointed Grumet, had in private agreed with Nadjari's attack on the Grumet report.

Lefkowitz, Nadjari's last defender and a fellow Republican, then issued a statement saying Nadjari was not telling the truth about their private conversation.

At his farewell press conference, Maurice Nadjari said: "I do not regret one single thing I said or did during the time I was special prosecutor."

October 17, 1977

4

Killing a City
and Killing a Sport

The piece on fire broker Joe Bald, and his gang of landlord-arsonists, was coauthored with Joe Conason, and with considerable assistance from fire marshal John Knox. We worked on it for more than six months, and four weeks after the piece was published, Bald and fourteen other people were indicted for arson and conspiracy in Brooklyn and the Bronx. In announcing the indictment, Brooklyn District Attorney Eugene Gold said that Bald and his coconspirators were "responsible for hundreds of buildings being burned for the insurance proceeds." Indicted with Bald were a political lawyer, a policeman, nine other landlords, and several "torches."

Bald subsequently plead guilty and became a government witness against many of his collaborators in the arson-for-profit racket.

"The Men Who Are Killing a Noble Sport" is also an attempt to personalize a general problem—boxing corruption—by naming the people I think are responsible. So far, law enforcement agencies have not followed up with criminal charges, as in the arson story, but I believe crimes have been committed by the rulers of boxing. The sport, as a system, as an institution, is venal from top to bottom, with few white hats, except the individuals I suggested at the end of the story for membership on a federal commission to regulate and reform boxing.

THE MEN WHO ARE BURNING
NEW YORK*

There are two crimes that are more than just felonies—they are
treason. One is the importation, distribution, and the sale of
heroin. The other is arson for profit.

These are not crimes of passion or desperation. They are
crimes of organized greed. They cause the deaths of innocent
citizens and brave firefighters. They kill blocks, ruin neighborhoods, and destroy cities. Ultimately, these are crimes that annul
hope and diminish humanity.

Arson breaks up families, frightens away investment and jobs,
and deprives the poor of housing. Every arsonist is potentially a
mass murderer. Those subversives who hire others to torch occu-
pied buildings—like those who move the envelopes of fine white
powder—are the first vultures of late capitalism.

It was more than two years ago that we first stumbled upon
this city's biggest arson ring of landlords, lawyers, brokers, and
insurance adjusters.

In the winter of 1978, the South Bronx was already a moonscape with abandoned, charcoaled shards. The cops who worked
in the forty-first precinct no longer called their station "Fort
Apache." They called it "The Little House on the Prairie," because there were so few surviving buildings or families in the area.

In the winter of 1978 the burning of the Bronx had moved
north into neighborhoods called Morris Heights, Morrisania, Tremont, Highbridge, Kingsbridge, and Fordham. Whenever there
was a suspicious fire and the homeless tenants were Hispanic or
black, the media would call the area the South Bronx. But it was
really other communities, and other police precincts.

For several days that winter we walked around these dying
blocks with a cop named Joe Dean, who was then assigned to the
Bronx arson task force in the forty-eighth precinct. We met not
only the most recent victims of arson, but those who feared they
would become tomorrow's refugees.

We saw tenants and small shopkeepers plead for protection,
saying the building next to them had burned the night before, and

*Written with Joe Conason.

that their house would be next. But because of budget cuts, neither the police nor the fire marshals nor the district attorney's office had the manpower to watch a building through the night.

Each day Joe Dean had to explain this to poor people who sensed they would soon be burned out for the second or third time in their lives. And Joe Dean felt powerless to do anything about it.

Within a week we saw the tenants of 201 Marcy Place, 1126 Kelly Street, and 1403 Grand Concourse turned into urban boat people by arson. And soon Dean was so frustrated by the suffering he saw—and could not stop—that he asked to be transferred to more risky plainclothes work in Times Square.

Eventually, we discovered a pattern to the burning of the Bronx, and later of Brooklyn, Manhattan, and Queens. Over the last five years, 250 buildings, all owned by one interlocking network of landlords—and all insured for large amounts—have had fires.

The maypole of this circle of landlords appears to be fifty-year-old Joe Bald, a convicted felon with ties to the Mafia. In 1978 we named Bald as one of the ten worst landlords in New York. Now he is about to go on trial in Queens for burning one rent-controlled building that he did not own. Other landlords affiliated with Bald in various realty companies, mortgages, transactions, deeds, partnerships, or fire insurance policies include Harry Rosen, Henry Katkin, Kenneth Passifiume, Marvin Siegel, Abe Sloan, Kenneth Aska, James Blackwell, and Benjamin Tabak.

Sometimes Bald's own name appears on the deed to a property. Sometimes the property is registered in the name of a front, frequently a superintendent or managing agent. Sometimes Bald only buys an interest in the mortgage. Sometimes the property is in the name of another landlord who has shared a dummy company with Bald in the past. Sometimes the property is never registered at all with the city.

Sometimes the building is in the name of fifty different shell companies that Bald uses, with names like Kajo Realty, 820 Suburban Realty Company, 952 Rehab Corporation, 748 St. Marks Development Corporation, or M.B. Management. Sometimes

Bald's interest in a property is completely hidden and is not on paper anywhere.

According to law enforcement agents, Bald even acts as a "fire broker" for other landlords. He will supply a torch for a building in which he has no financial interest—for a fee or a future consideration.

But there is always the extraordinary coincidence of fire and money, of arson and insurance. There is the pattern of the building bought, the swift withdrawal of heat and hot water from the tenants, and then the fire set in the middle of the night in a top rear apartment.

Over the last five years, Bald and a variety of his associates have collected an estimated $5 million in fire insurance claims. Bald's properties have been insured by Lloyd's of London, by the FAIR plan, and by other private companies.

Despite Bald's indictment for arson last September in Queens, he seems to be as active as ever. Three buildings purchased by Bald this year around the Grand Concourse have already had a series of fires, and are now abandoned. One of these buildings is 55 East 175th Street—a six-floor, brick apartment house acquired in January of 1980 by 446 Management Corporation, in which Bald holds a financial interest. This large, decent building had two suspicious fires on March 3, another on March 4, another on April 27, and a fifth fire on May 11. It now stands empty, the roof gone, the windows broken, mounds of burnt garbage in the courtyard.

We have spent thirty months trying to piece this story together, not merely to name these urban traitors but also to explore and explain why whole neighborhoods of this city have been put to the torch. The idea that tenants set most of these fires themselves in order to qualify for public housing—or that vandals or street gangs set them—is a myth. The fact is that landlords set the fires in order to collect insurance money.

And, for years, the insurance industry has not cared. The fire insurance underwriters have simply passed the costs of arson along to the public in the form of higher and higher rates.

Joe Bald's operations span the city, from Harlem to the Grand Concourse, from Bed-Stuy to Far Rockaway, but his chief place of business is Room 703, 16 Court Street, Brooklyn. His name is on the door, beneath the heading Real Estate, along with the names of two other companies and three individuals.

Inside Bald's suite is a tiny waiting area, shut off by a locked door from the actual offices. A secretary peers from behind a window, making the operation look more like a ghetto check-cashing service than a real estate firm. But Bald hasn't been spending much time in the office lately; believing, perhaps, that his phone is tapped, Joe Bald has been making a lot of calls from the pay phones downstairs on Court Street.

Bald's career is somewhat opaque. Over the past ten years he has been identified as a rabbi, a furniture dealer, an interior decorator, a landlord, and a management agent. What's known for certain is that arson for profit was not his first criminal business.

According to Michael Hellerman's autobiographical *Wall Street Swindler,* Bald was instrumental in several Hellerman-masterminded stock fraud schemes involving top organized crime figures. Bald is portrayed as a mere tool in these transactions, most of which took place in 1970 and 1971.

When Hellerman decided to handle a stock swindle involving a mob-connected New Jersey car-leasing firm, he used Bald as a front and go-between. Among the "investors" in this rip-off were mobsters Vinnie Aloi, John "Dio" Dioguardi, and Vincent Lombardo, son-in-law of crime genius Meyer Lansky.

Some time later, when Hellerman needed a place to cash checks he was collecting in a bigger stock manipulation, he went to Bald again. "Bald was a man of many contacts," wrote Hellerman, "and the check cashiers he came up with were a couple of rabbis who worked in the New York Jewelry Exchange. Bald assured me that the rabbis were reliable men, willing to cash the checks for us, no questions asked. . . ." Hellerman decided to swindle the rabbis, too, but Bald apparently betrayed him out of fear. The rabbis retaliated by kidnapping one of Hellerman's associates and holding him prisoner for three days, until Bald produced enough second mortgages and cash to secure his release.

None of this made the papers, and it's entirely possible that Bald's Queens neighbors thought of him simply as a good family man with mysterious business activities. But in November 1970 Bald was implicated in the Imperial Investment Corporation fraud case along with Hellerman, New York mob boss Carmine Tramunti, Aloi, Dioguardi, and Lombardo. Shortly before the indictments came down, Bald, his brother-in-law Harold Blond, a Democratic fundraiser named Edward Adams, and an aide to Republican Senator Hiram Fong of Hawaii began seeking ways to fix the Imperial case. But neither Bald nor his associates realized that Hellerman had long since become an FBI informant. Before an undercover agent blew it open, the bribery attempt had been carried to the point where Fong aide Robert Carson offered $100,000 to Deputy Attorney General Richard Kleindienst. Bald pleaded not guilty when the bribery arrests were first made. But by November 1971, when the case went to trial, he had changed his plea to guilty. Though he never directly fingered the organized crime investors, Bald testified that "we offered a million dollars if the Imperial Investment Corporation matter could be taken care of."

Thanks to his somewhat cooperative testimony, Bald only got a few months in jail. Not counting a brief furlough to attend his son's bar mitzvah, Bald spent three months in Danbury federal prison, and entered the world of real estate upon his release in May 1972.

Joe Bald is at the center of a group of fire-prone landlords, some of whom have been his partners in front corporations, others who have merely sold Bald buildings to dispose of as best he could.

Kenneth Passafiume, Bald's partner in Nony Realty and Kajo Realty, was perhaps his closest associate. Kajo-owned buildings had at least twenty-one fires deemed suspicious, incendiary, or unknown between April 1976 and August 1977. The modus operandi was simple. A twenty-eight-unit building at 161 Clarkson Avenue in Flatbush was bought by Bald and Passafiume in April 1976, and services were cut off to the tenants; repairs went undone, and homes went unheated until, in late summer, the suspicious fires began. Finally, over a two-week period in December, two larger fires broke out. Bald and Passafiume collected $15,200 from the FAIR plan, a state-run insurance pool, and a few months later the building was sealed. By March 1977, Bald and Passafiume were applying for a low-cost city loan to "rehabilitate" 161 Clarkson.

Passafiume, who lived in New Jersey while his Brooklyn properties burned, ignored at least one court order directing him to make repairs at 161 Clarkson. His previous record shows two arrests: one in 1975 for possession of a gun and "menacing," and another in 1977 for drunk driving.

A second Bald associate, more respectable at first glance, is Henry Katkin, a Brooklyn landlord whose city tax arrears once reached $170,000. Katkin and Bald own at least two buildings together, one recorded under the bizarre name of Terrain Renewal. Located at 280 East Ninety-first Street in Brooklyn, the building had two fires of unknown origin within three weeks in late 1976. The second building, at 350 Pennsylvania Avenue in East New York, had a fire of unknown origin a month earlier. The insurable loss on the two buildings totaled $37,000.

One of the most active of Bald's associates is Marvin Siegel, with whom he has done business under the corporate name of Sagamore Realty. Over a period of eight months in 1977, Siegel bought up at least a dozen properties in the South Bronx for nominal cash. Then, on February 22, 1978, he turned them over to Bald, again for a nominal consideration. On paper, these properties were worth about $350,000 in all. Each one has since had a serious fire of suspicious origin, and three—at 1173 West Farms Road, 1126 Kelly Street, and 559 Southern Boulevard—were burned to the ground. According to law enforcement authorities, all of these buildings were insured for amounts far in excess of their assessed valuation or the amount Bald's companies paid for them. Nearly all of them were in tax arrears.

Landlords don't burn buildings themselves in most cases, although sometimes the "torch" will also be used as a front man to disguise a building's ownership.

Joe Bald's favorite torches appear to be Kenneth Aska, Richard Payne, James Blackwell, and Ralph Turane. These four men, all considerably younger than Bald, will soon go on trial with him for the incendiary fires at 750 Empire Avenue in Queens.

Aska, who has also gone under the aliases of Kenneth Brooks and Alvin Donnelly, was born in New York thirty-one years ago and now lives in the pleasant suburb of Central Islip. He drives a white 1978 Lincoln Mark V, and reportedly owns three other cars. He lists his occupation as "investment consultant" and his business address as "820 Realty, 1727 Townsend Avenue, Bronx."

Seventeen twenty-seven Townsend is owned by one Joseph Bene-dicke, who shares Bald's business address at 16 Court Street, and shares a business phone with Joseph Mayer, Bald's partner in a front outfit called M.B. Management Corporation. The building at nearby 820 Suburban Place, which was taken by the city for nonpayment of taxes in 1978 (and to which the name 820 Realty refers) was owned by M.B. Management.

Aska's offices were raided by the police on September 20, 1979, the same day he was arrested for arson and conspiracy in the burning of 750 Empire Avenue. Among the papers taken from his office was a long list of buildings located in the Bronx, Brooklyn, and Manhattan, some of which have suffered serious fires. Also collated from materials found at the office was a list of property owners or managers who have done business with 820 Realty, and whose properties have been investigated by the Fire Department for suspected arson.

Among these landlords are Benjamin Tabak and Harry Rosen, who have been sued many times for violations of tenant rights and inhumane behavior. Tabak, who owns properties in Williams-burg, was almost arrested in 1977 for failing to appear in court to answer tenant charges against him. He was also one of the *Voice*'s "ten worst landlords" of 1978. Those tenants told the *Voice* that, along with no heat or hot water and no effort to correct 200 violations of the building code, there were four suspi-cious fires during Tabak's effort to drive them out of their homes at 184 Grand Street. (While collecting rents from these tenants, Tabak didn't bother to pay any property taxes to the city.) The religious organization used by Tabak as a front for his ownership of 184 Grand Street also appears in the group of names found at Aska's office.

Harry Rosen is an old-timer; we have been told that one of the first court cases ever filed by the city for housing code viola-tions was against Rosen. But such efforts by the city don't seem to have affected him much: in November 1978, after a two-year court battle with city authorities over hazardous conditions in two of his Brooklyn buildings, Rosen and his partner Sam Biller were fined $4000 for contempt by a civil court judge.

Law enforcement sources believe Aska and his associates were running a sort of arson service business out of their offices at 1727

Townsend. Aska himself has been arrested on two previous occasions. In 1971 he and his brother-in-law Richard Payne were charged with grand larceny and coercion, or causing fear of injury to a person or property. The following year he was arrested on a misdemeanor charge of "obstructing governmental administration." Both of these cases arose out of Aska's involvement with Black Economist Survival, a group of black Bronx construction workers whose leader, James Sims, was convicted of extortion in 1975. The charges against Aska and Payne were ultimately dropped.

Aska—a tough guy who tried to kick a *Voice* photographer last week and later threatened violence against him—appears to be the most senior of Bald's helpers. He knew enough about arson mythology to accuse an elderly Jewish tenant leader of setting the fires at 750 Empire Avenue when he, Aska, was arrested for that crime last September.

Last week in Queens Supreme Court we saw the defendants in the 750 Empire case for the first time. They were brought to Judge John Leagy's courtroom in handcuffs, having spent the previous evening in jail. Though the five of them were originally released on $50,000 bail each, they'd spent the night behind bars because of an incident in the courthouse hallway the day before. After a pretrial hearing, Bald, the attorney representing him, and the other defendants were waiting for an elevator. Standing next to them was Queens Assistant District Attorney Joseph Maddalone, who says that Bald began making "smart remarks" in his direction about "letters being sent to the judge." Maddalone says he asked Bald's attorney, Arnold Weiss—who happens to be a former Democratic reform leader from Manhattan—to "control his client." Weiss' response was: "Tell it to the judge."

That's what Maddalone did, and the five defendants' bail was temporarily revoked. We watched them apologize humbly to Maddalone and the judge in the courtroom the next day. The judge reinstated their bail, and they left.

The tension in that courtroom reflects just how "hot" this particular arson case has become. The building which burned was a site of community controversy for more than a year before it was set on fire with flammable liquids and a road flare. Far Rockaway is undergoing convulsions much feared by its middle-class residents, who focused on 750 Empire Avenue as a symbol of local deterioration. According to documents in possession of the former tenants, a nonprofit corporation was formed by members of a local temple, Kneseth Israel, to buy the building and demolish it so that one- and two-family homes could be built on the site.

The dummy corporation which took over the building in November 1978 was called Golem—in Yiddish, "monster"—Realty Corporation. According to law enforcement sources, the real owner was Dorn Management, whose president Mordechai Sohn is also the president of Temple Kneseth Israel. Because the new owners refused to provide heat or services, the twenty tenants remaining in the forty-eight-unit structure often withheld their rent. Between January and March of 1979, the complex suffered four incendiary blazes, the fires for which Bald and company were indicted on counts of arson and conspiracy.

Bald's relationship to this particular set of fires is exceptional, and in a way it's ironic that he is finally being prosecuted for this case. From the doorway of 739 Elvira Avenue in Far Rockaway, where Bald has lived for many years with his wife and children, he could see 750 Empire Avenue. He is a respectable member of his community and of Temple Kneseth Israel. The irony of the case is that Bald and his cronies are about to be tried for a crime that may have been a favor to friends in the neighborhood, friends who have accomplished their goal without being caught. Bald may find time to ponder this in prison.

It is also possible that he may not go to prison again. Few arsonists are convicted, particularly when they have lawyers as skilled as those representing Bald and Aska.

Aside from Bald's deep involvement with mob-linked stock swindles ten years ago, the clearest signals of organized-crime involvement in the arson plague are Bald and Aska's lawyers. Though ex-reformer Arnold Weiss appeared for Bald in court last week, he did it only as a favor to Bald's busy attorney of record, Jay Goldberg.

Goldberg is a Harvard Law graduate, who once worked for Attorney General Robert Kennedy on racketeering cases in Indiana. He is now a prosperous mob lawyer. For a brief period in the mid-sixties, Goldberg used his gangbuster reputation to seek reform Democratic support for assembly and district attorney races in the Bronx. Now, having represented several top mob figures as a criminal defender since those days, Goldberg is defending a landlord who has helped to destroy the Bronx. Among Goldberg's organized crime clients are Vinnie Aloi, Johnny Dio, Carmine Galante, Matty "the Horse" Ianniello, the brothers Anthony "Tony Pro" and Salvatore Provenzano, the late porn boss Michael Zaffarno, and porno lawyer Seymour Detsky.

Aska's attorney is Herbert Lyons, another high-priced criminal lawyer. Lyons's most celebrated client was former Brooklyn congressman Frank Brasco who, despite Lyons's talents, was convicted of taking a bribe from a mobster.

People who study arson disagree about motive. Some believe most arsons are motivated by revenge, insanity, or thrill seeking. Another popular notion is that poor people burn their own homes so that welfare agencies will help them move to better housing. But we've never heard a professional fire investigator say that less than 25 percent of all arsons were set for profit.

Our knowledge of arson is limited, in substantial part, because the biggest insurance companies have done so little about the problem. Though arsonists make millions by defrauding insurance companies, the corporate response has been less than overwhelming. The companies are naturally concerned with covering their own assets first—which means worrying more about lawsuits for disclosure of insurance data to law enforcement agencies or for withholding fire claims in suspicious circumstances—than about the social problem of arson. The insurance industry is very big on recommendations, advisory committees, generalized research, and conference discussions; it's short on action. The industry's lethargy may have something to do with its ability to redline threatened neighborhoods and, when too many losses threaten profits, to raise fire insurance rates on all residential buildings. This approach leaves much to be desired, since the solutions penalize honest homeowners and tenants much more than they hamper crooks.

One problem is that most insurance companies do little investigation of properties on their own before insuring them. Lloyd's of London, which has reportedly been victimized by arson fraud in New York and elsewhere, has just begun to probe some of its fire claims, but only after enormous losses.

And there seems to be clear evidence that at least some insurance claims adjusters are in league with the arsonists. Others may simply turn a blind eye to suspicious evidence. The *Voice* has learned, for example, that Bald's insurance adjuster has continued to settle claims on his properties long after Bald was indicted for arson.

Without some cooperation or willful ignorance on the part of insurers, how could landlords insure properties for hundreds of thousands of dollars more than the purchase price or assessed value? One law enforcement agent told us privately that he believes insurance agents are actually running the Bronx and Brooklyn arson rackets. But because it is so difficult to convict a torch, let alone a landlord, it's hard to "flip" a witness who will testify against insurance adjusters—or mob figures—in court.

Arson is the cremation ritual of a diseased housing system. A striking fact for anyone who tours a New York neighborhood ravaged by arson and abandonment is that there are still many people living there—in public housing. The private sector has been unable to create an attractive level of profit from low-income housing (without subsidies or tax shelters) for decades. In part, this has been caused by the fact that the poor and working poor still lack the income to pay higher rents. In part, it has been caused by the continuing lack of sufficient income for the poor and working poor to pay higher rents. (Contrary to neoconservative mythology, these problems have *not* been caused by rent controls: they exist in cities without rent controls, and the situation is worst in neighborhoods where rent-control prices would be well above market levels.)

There is simply no incentive for banks, landlords, insurance companies, or anyone else with money to invest in building or rebuilding dwellings at reasonable rents. So landlords are encouraged to let their low-income housing fall apart until they've milked the last dollar of rent and evaded every dollar of taxes. Ultimately, the easiest and most lucrative step is to burn the housing, or sell it to someone else who will burn it. In housing, the final stage of capitalism is arson.

June 2, 1980

THE MEN WHO ARE KILLING A NOBLE SPORT

Why do fighters die in the ring? Who is at fault? The referee? The manager? The promoter? The winning fighter? Should boxing be abolished? Should boxers wear protective headguards? Should all bouts be limited to ten rounds? Should the gloves be padded? Can prefight physicals be more exacting?

In the aftermath of the death of South Korean lightweight Duk-Koo Kim, these questions are being asked again. When Kim died, I was in the midst of preparing a long investigative article about professional boxing. In the meantime, I have some tentative thoughts about the sport, about the circumstances that might contribute to a fatality, about the institutional arrangements of boxing, and about what might be done to clean up our most corrupt sport.

Bob Arum, the promoter of the Ray Mancini–Duk-Koo Kim bout, was also the promoter of a boxing card held on September 30 aboard the U.S.S. *Yorktown,* in Charleston, South Carolina. South Carolina does not have a state boxing commission to regulate the sport, only a city commission with the lowest possible standards of competency for licensing, medical exams, and record keeping. Arum's September 30 promotion was televised into a potential market of nineteen million homes by ESPN, the all-sports cable television network.

The semifinal bout was between undefeated Billy Collins and "Raheem Tayib," who was said to have an 11 to 6 record as a professional boxer. But "Raheem Tayib" was, in fact, an imposter, a ringer using a phony Islamic name. His real name was Eddie Flanning. *And Flanning had been knocked out in his last five consecutive fights, all within three rounds.* Flanning had been knocked out six days earlier, under his real name in Madison Square Garden, by hard-punching José "The Threat" Baret. Flanning was fighting in South Carolina under an assumed name and falsified record, despite a mandatory sixty-day medical suspension he received as a result of his Madison Square knockout.

Randy Gordon was the ESPN commentator on the night of the Collins-"Tayib" farce. Gordon, a young associate editor at

Ring Magazine and a former amateur boxer, is more knowledgeable and candid than some of the famous network boxing an-
nouncers. Gordon says when a decision stinks, when a fighter is
a stiff, when a bout is boring.

At the weigh-in, Gordon recognized that "Tayib" was really
Flanning. He confronted the boxer and told him he knew his true
identity. Gordon also informed Akbar Muhammad, the executive
vice-president of Arum's Top Rank Promotions, who was in
Charleston, that he felt an ethical obligation as a journalist to
disclose "Tayib"'s real name on the air. Gordon told Muhammad
that he could either find another opponent for Collins, or cancel
the bout entirely.

The Collins-"Tayib" fight was a brutal mismatch. "Tayib"
moaned from the body punches he absorbed. His mouth and nose
were bloodied. He was knocked down in the second round after
three uppercuts, and finally knocked out in the third round.

During the bout Randy Gordon, to his everlasting credit,
informed the viewers that "Tayib" appeared to be Flanning, but
that "Tayib" denied it vehemently. It was only after Gordon
returned to New York, saw the tape of the Baret fight, and saw
the photo of Flanning on his New York boxing license, that he
was positive he was right.

Three weeks later, Scotty Connal, ESPN's executive vice-
president, fired Randy Gordon, insisting the termination had
absolutely nothing to do with Gordon exposing Arum's fiasco in
Charleston.

ESPN has a two-year contract with Arum to televise fights
that Top Rank promotes, but does not have its own "quality
control" boxing expert to evaluate the competitiveness of these
fights, the way the three major networks do. Arum has an unusual
amount of control and freedom with ESPN.

Arum maintains that he had nothing to do with the firing of
Randy Gordon by ESPN, and that the timing of the dismissal was
pure coincidence. But Gordon has been told by several Arum
associates that Arum was responsible for his firing. Also, on the
night of the Collins-"Tayib" hoax, *New York Times* boxing writer
Michael Katz phoned Arum at home and spoke to him. According to Katz, Arum told him: "Randy should be careful what he
says. He can get into trouble."

Stan Isaacs, TV sports columnist for *Newsday*, has written: "Despite denials by ESPN and Arum, the boxing cognoscenti believe the promoter helped influence the cable network to dump Gordon."

What happened on ESPN possibly was a federal crime. Someone at Top Rank knowingly put a boxer on the air under an assumed name and a false record, while that boxer was under medical suspension. But worse than a potential felony, it was a potential tragedy. Eddie Flanning could have been killed.

The WBA (World Boxing Association), based in Panama, and the WBC (World Boxing Council), based in Mexico City, are the two international groups that publish monthly ratings of boxers and sanction title fights. They are both universally regarded as venal vessels easily manipulated by a few promoters and managers. The greed, cynicism, anti-American bias, and conflicts of interest of each were documented in two excellent articles by Pat Putnam in *Sports Illustrated* last year. José Sulaimin, president of the WBC, is under indictment in Mexico for smuggling artifacts.

Atrium's rival, Don King, has a close relationship with the WBC, while Arum's connections to the WBA are so cozy that some boxing insiders joke that the initials WBA signify With Bob's Approval. The WBA and WBC should be independent regulators of boxing; they are, in fact, complicit connivers in rigging ratings. Internally they are both dominated by ruthless shadow men in Panama, Mexico, Puerto Rico, and South Africa.

In every division except middleweight (Marvin Hagler) and welterweight (vacant with the retirement of Ray Leonard), the WBA and WBC recognize different champions. This is ideal for the voracious appetite of television, which can truthfully sell twenty-nine different boxers in sixteen different weight classifications as "world champions." Boxing gets great ratings on TV. Every weekend TV can now buy the rights to a mismatch that claims to be for some artificial title, from WBC cruiserweight to WBA superbantamweight. The sponsors just want to be able to advertise that the fight is for some championship, even if it is only a cardboard crown concocted by Arum and CBS, or King and ABC.

The Mancini-Kim fight was for the WBA lightweight title,

because the WBA somehow rated Kim the number one contender. Historically, the WBA ratings system has unduly inflated
the standing of boxers from two tyrannies—South Africa and
South Korea. In the current WBA rankings Sang Hyun Kim of
South Korea is rated the number one challenger for Aaron Pryor's
junior welterweight title. Soon Hyun Chung is rated the number
one challenger for Leonardo Cruz, the junior featherweight
champion; Hwan Kil Yuh is rated the number two challenger to
featherweight titlist Eusebio Pedroza; Sung Nam Kim is rated the
number one contender for the junior flyweight title; and Kim was
rated the number one lightweight contender, ahead of much
more skilled fighters like Howard Davis and Edwin Rosario. It was
on the basis of this unearned rating that Kim was given a chance
to fight for the title, and partially on the basis of this rating that
CBS paid Arum about $300,000 for the rights to televise the bout.
(Kim only got $20,000 for his last fight!) CBS has, in fact, pur-
chased all of Mancini's fights for the last two years from Arum.

After Kim was knocked out and lapsed into his terminal coma,
Mort Sharnick, the CBS boxing consultant, justifying his corporate decision to buy the fight, told the *Times:* "There is always
prejudice in North America against foreign fighters."

This is Orwellian Newspeak. It is American fighters—blacks
and Latins—who are the victims of the politicized ratings. Marvin Hagler and Aaron Pryor should have become champions years
before they did, except they were kept out of the number one
contender spot by chicanery. Hagler, who was already the best
middleweight in the world, was excluded from Don King's scan-
dalous tournament on ABC in 1977 because he lacked connections. And Pryor had to seek the junior welterweight belt because
no lightweight champion would fight him. Today, Howard Davis,
with a record of twenty-one wins and one defeat, is not even rated
among the top ten lightweights by the WBA. (Davis is a former
New York Golden Gloves champ and 1976 Olympic Champion.)

In contrast, through influence, gifts, gratuities, favors, payoffs,
or whatever, stiffs from foreign lands have repeatedly been given
chances to compete for world titles. The stupendously inept Korean Young Ho O was knocked out by Hilmer Kenty. The stupendously inept Lorenzo Zanon of Italy was knocked out by Larry
Holmes in a heavyweight title fight. The stupendously inept Er-
nesto Espana of Puerto Rico (managed by the unsavory ex-convict

Pepi Cordero) had four title fights, and lost them all, the last one to Ray Mancini. The stupendously inept Fulgencio Obelmejias of Venezuela has been knocked out twice in a row by Marvin Hagler in middleweight title bouts.

The two most impartial and reliable ratings of boxers are compiled by *Ring Magazine* and the International Boxing Writers Association. *Ring Magazine*'s ratings are based on the combined judgments of a worldwide panel of fifty experts, including two Koreans. The most recent edition of *Ring Magazine* did not rate Kim among the top ten lightweights in the world. The top five were: Pryor, Mancini, Rosario, Davis, and Andy Ganigan, which is exactly how I would evaluate them.

The International Boxing Writers Association rankings, based on a poll of fifteen of the most informed boxing writers, does not have Kim in the top ten and has never ranked him among the ten best lightweights in the world. Michael Katz, the boxing writer for *The New York Times*, says he would not have judged Kim among the top fifteen lightweights in the world before the Mancini bout.

Ray "Boom Boom" Mancini is the rarest and most valuable commodity in all of boxing, a white champion. He is the only one. More than that, he is a genuinely likable, charismatic twenty-one-year-old, and unlike Gerry Cooney, he can really fight.

Bob Arum has Mancini tied up in an exclusive, multifight contract with options for CBS, just as Don King has Larry Holmes under an exclusive long-term contract. It was in Arum's financial interest as the TV packager that Mancini keep the title and keep winning, while CBS and the rest of the medium built him up into a star attraction of the magnitude of Ray Leonard. So Arum fed him an unqualified challenger named Kim, who was not a legitimate threat to his commodity. Because Kim was well trained and had extraordinary desire, the bout itself seemed competitive in a limited sense. Mancini won most of the rounds and was far ahead in the scoring, but all the rounds were close and exciting until the fatal end. And Arum had already lined up another mediocre club fighter named Ken "Bang Bang" Bogner to be Mancini's next safe opponent, although Bogner was also unranked by *Ring,* and was much less deserving of a title opportunity than, say, Howard Davis.

As Kim lay brain-dead in a Las Vegas Hospital the day after

the fight, Arum solemnly called for a two-month moritorium on all professional boxing in America, while a blue-ribbon committee of medical experts studied ways to improve safety. What Arum neglected to mention was that he has no major promotions scheduled for the next two months, while his competitor, Don King, has three big fights planned, including Holmes and Tex Cobb this Friday, and Wilfred Benitez and Thomas Hearns on December 3.

Arum has acquired a more benign public image than Don King. He is, after all, a former federal prosecutor, while King is a former prison inmate. But Arum has no better morals. He is a cutthroat businessman with little respect for fighters themselves. He has promoted some of the most cynical mismatches in history, ranging from Marvin Hagler's sixty-seven-second knockout of Caveman Lee, to Evel Knievel's defeat by the Snake River. He is now getting fights for the pathetic, washed-up Roberto Duran. He has financed some of his promotions with money supplied by the Southern Sun hotel and casino chain in South Africa. Five fighters—including undefeated Johnny Bumphus and Tony Ayala —have sued Arum for secretly assigning their television rights to NBC without their knowledge or consent. This covert and monopolistic practice prevented the boxers from being free agents—selling their services to the highest bidder among the three networks. And Jim Jacobs, one of the most honorable men in boxing, is also suing Arum for trying to steal his champion, Wilfred Benitez, from him.

"The trouble with suing Arum," Jacobs says, "is that you have to stand in line."

Boxing is the sport most vulnerable to corruption. The profits to be made from television and closed circuit are now astronomical. Professional racketeers and gamblers have been entrenched in the sport since the 1920s. Boxing is an unstructured, anarchistic sport. There are no regular schedules or leagues; who fights who is improvised and arbitrary. The standings are political. There is no central repository of records or results. Most state commissions are filled with political appointees. There is no strong credible monitoring authority as in baseball, football, or basketball. Even the scoring of each fight is purely subjective.

The casual conflicts of interest in boxing are mind-boggling.

A Sean O'Grady fight two years ago was refereed by Champ Thomas, the author of a book called: *Sean O'Grady: Living Legend*. When Ayub Kalule boxed Ray Leonard in 1981, one of Kalule's handlers was a Dane named Ove Ovesen, the same man who was a judge in 1979 when Kalule boxed Steve Gregory. Ovesen voted 150 to 134 for his friend Kalule, giving him every round. Another judge, from South Africa, gave the fight to Kalule by just three points.

Nevertheless, boxing still holds a powerful ambivalent appeal for me. And for many of my friends. And for many writers of humanitarian sympathy. Albert Camus was a boxing fan whose superb account of a club fight in Oran, Algeria, is collected in his *Lyrical and Critical Essays*, alongside his intellectual opposition to violence and capital punishment. Camus's essay ends: "At Corinth, two temples stood side by side—the Temple of Violence, the Temple of Necessity."

I still find watching a film of Sugar Ray Robinson as exhilarating as reading a poem by Yeats, listening to a spiritual sung by Mahalia Jackson, or hearing a soliloquy composed by Shakespeare. Artistry is artistry, regardless of the calling.

On November 14 the *Times* published an editorial suggesting the abolition of boxing, comparing it to public hangings. The *Times* appears to be even more ambivalent about violence than Camus, since the paper has also editorialized against the movement for a verifiable, mutual freeze on nuclear weapons by the United States and Soviet Union. I've always thought the MX could inflict more damage than the one-two.

The more appropriate response to the present introspection about boxing would be a restructuring of the sport, the purging of all corrupt, monopolistic elements. This would start with the acceptance that boxing can no longer police itself.

The WBA and WBC are essentially instruments of extortion that make up their own rules. They exist only because of the money from American television networks. CBS, NBC, and ABC are the principal financiers of boxing, along with Caesars Palace Casino for some of the megabouts. If the networks simply stopped recognizing the legitimacy of the WBA and WBC, that would break their stranglehold on the sport. The TV networks could announce tomorrow that they will only recognize the ratings published by *Ring* as legitimate, and use those to sanction all championship fights. The way it works now, money from American TV advertisers subsidizes the WBC and WBA, which, in turn, discriminate against American boxers.

To fill the void this would create, a strong federal boxing commission should be created by an act of Congress. This federal commission could set medical standards for boxers, require life and health insurance and a pension system partially financed by the TV networks, computerize all fighters' records to avoid imposters like Eddie Flanning, upgrade doctor and referee training, grade all boxers to avoid flagrant mismatches, and have all necessary powers of enforcement, including license revocation.

There are no factions of "good guys" and "bad guys" in boxing. The "outs" are as bad as the "ins." Arum and King, the WBC and WBA, are equally evil. But there are individuals of integrity I would trust to sit on a federal regulatory commission: managers Jim Jacobs, Cus D'Amato, and Mike Trainer; writers Pat Putnam and Michael Katz; trainer Ray Arcel; *Ring Magazine* editor Bert Sugar; ex-fighters Sugar Ray Leonard, José Torres, and Emile Griffith, now an excellent trainer.

Boxing incorporates the duality of Dickens—the best of times and the worst of times, the season of light and the season of darkness, the epoch of belief and the epoch of incredulity. For every mismatch, there is the glory of Ali and Frazier in Manila. For every unjust rating, there is the nobility of Arguello and Pryor. For every Lorenzo Zanon, there is the memory of Ray Robinson. For every Bob Arum and Don King there is a kid with a dream in a ghetto going to a gym instead of to jail.

The Temple of Violence *was* next to the Temple of Necessity at Corinth.
November 30, 1982

5

Are There Second Acts After Camelot?

These two pieces are joined because they suggest how complex and unpredictable life can be. Ted Sorensen and Bill Moyers were both part of Camelot. Sorensen was the friend of, adviser to, and speechwriter for John Kennedy. Moyers was friend, adviser, and aide to Lyndon Johnson.

At an unusually young age each tasted enormous power. But they lost that power early in life, when they ceased to work for the President of the United States.

These two pieces are really about Second Acts in American lives—of which Scott Fitzgerald said there were none. Sorensen took a traditional path from Camelot: he wrote a book about JFK, and he helped mythologize him in a cloying fashion; he ran for the Senate and lost; and then he became a successful corporate lawyer, and a Democratic party insider.

Moyers took a harder route. He never wrote a book abut LBJ; he never cashed in on his insider's knowledge. He created a career for himself in television, and grew in his second act to become the best in America at what he did. He became the second coming of Edward R. Murrow.

Moyers has found a way to keep his populist moralism intact, while becoming an artistic success inside the corporate world. No one could have predicted this fifteen years ago. And some might have wrongly foreseen such a future for Sorensen.

TED SORENSEN: A BURNT-OUT CASE

The thing wrong with Theodore Sorensen is the thing wrong with American politics.

The thing is not easy to distill into a few words. It is an elusive mix of personal ambition divorced from values or passion or ideas, old-fashioned venality, and a huckster's cynical obsession with technique and media image making. All of which is covered over by the most reasonable public rhetoric no sane person could disagree with. It is the invisibility of evil, the concealment of character.

So first, a few raw facts about Theodore Chaiken Sorensen.

In 1967, Sorensen advised Robert Kennedy not to speak out against the bombing of North Vietnam because it might harm his career. In 1966, Sorensen accepted a large legal fee to represent General Motors against the consumer's tribune, Ralph Nader. Also as a lawyer, Sorensen went to work for the statewide association of doctors who tried to discredit and sabotage the state's Medicaid program of free medical care for the indigent. At the 1968 Democratic convention, Sorensen, while publicly aligned with the antiwar delegates, worked secretly in hotel rooms and on telephones for Hubert Humphrey, and tried to undercut the doves during the peace plank fight.

But those are just the big political things. There are also the little things, the little flashes into a man's character.

There is Sorensen, tortuously rationalizing and justifying John F. Kennedy's Vietnam policies in his book *Kennedy*, published in 1965, now telling audiences, "I didn't have anything to do with foreign policy when I served President Kennedy." There is Sorensen taking out full-page newspaper ads during the recent epidemic of ghetto heroin deaths, implying his opponents have ignored the problem while he has been working hard on it for years. There is Sorensen flying to Moscow on the eve of Passover to score cheap political points with New York's Jewish voters by having the remarkable courage to attack Soviet anti-Semitism. There is Sorensen giving inspirational sermons about moral clarity in times of crises, and then trying to explain away his failure to endorse John Lindsay against Mario Procaccino, or explain why he pleaded with Robert Kennedy not to run in 1968. There is Sorensen writing Ted Kennedy's wretched television speech after Chappaquiddick, and then, when it didn't wash, going on the David Frost television show to deny he ever wrote it and claiming his only role at Hyannis Port was "preventing mistatements of fact." There is Sorensen, quoting the Kennedys, writing books about the Kennedys, trying to link his name to their magic, but ask anyone who works full-time in any cause, in any movement in the country what Sorensen has done to help them even privately, and the answer is always "nothing." Talk to the antiwar organizers or the welfare rights organization, talk to the Young Lords, talk to the grape strikers, ask Dr. Spock, Bill Kunstler, Jesse Jackson, Saul Alinsky, or Ralph Nader, ask anyone who really spends his or her life working for change, and they will all tell you they have no use for Sorensen.

I don't know of any other figure in American politics whose public reputation and real worth are at such variance. To suburban housewives in Huntington who have time only to read the *Nation* once a week, to upstate county leaders who have only heard about him by reputation, to journeymen reporters based in Moscow who have never actually met him, Sorensen symbolizes the paradise lost of the New Frontier: social reform, style, idealism, wit, intelligence.

But those professionals who know Sorensen, who have worked day-to-day with him, who have sat in meetings with him and drafted statements with him, or those seasoned political journalists who have observed him closely over a decade—to them Sorensen is an imposter. Just as you had to *know* Robert Kennedy to appreciate him, you have to *know* Sorensen to be appalled by him.

Dun Gifford until recently was on Ted Kennedy's Washington staff. In 1968, he worked in Robert Kennedy's campaign. He knows Sorensen very well. Usually a bright staff man like Gifford will not talk on the record about a colleague like Sorensen. But Gifford feels the responsibility to share his insider's knowledge, the urge to correct the mistaken image.

"Sorensen," Gifford says, "has an infatuation with technique. He only cares about the appearances of things. He is a great technician. He knows how to write a speech in an hour that will

make 6000 steelworkers applaud. He knows how to draft a letter
to De Gaulle that will please all sides. And I have a great respect
for this skill. But I have never seen him show any emotion about
any cause or any issue. He has a love of management. What he
knows best is how to put a cosmetic on any situation, how to make
up the best excuse."

Jeff Greenfield also got to know Sorensen as a comrade when
they worked side by side in Robert Kennedy's truncated 1968
campaign. Greenfield says, "Ted Sorensen reminds me of Richard
Nixon. His speeches never look you in the eye and tell you what's
really going on. They always twist the truth. . . . He has a
fascination with power in a tight-assed way, just like Nixon. Sorensen believes in manipulation rather than participation. . . .
Sorensen will never admit he was wrong. Bobby admitted he was
wrong on Vietnam and shouldered all the blame. But Sorensen's
basic skill is that of a rhetorician, at papering over real differences
with phony language. He uses words as a gimmick. His hang-up
on alliteration indicates how he only cares about gimmicks and
not the guts of anything."

Fred Dutton worked in the White House with Sorensen during the early 1960s, and worked closely with him in the 1968
campaign. He says, "When I first came into the White House in
1961, I had heard that Ted Sorensen was the great liberal intellectual. But in practice, it was Ken O'Donnell, who was supposed
to be the cold Irish pol, who would push on civil rights, who would
ask 'is it good for people?' while Sorensen would always ask, 'is it
smart politics?' "

Peter Maas, author of *The Valachi Papers*, has been close to
the Kennedys for almost ten years. He knew Bobby when he was
Attorney General. He covered Kennedy's 1964 Senate campaign
in New York. He has watched Sorensen operate in public and
private for a long time. "Ted Sorensen is pathetic," Maas says.
"He is totally used up. In the speech he wrote for Teddy after
Chappaquiddick, he lifted three paragraphs right out of *Profiles
in Courage*. And then at Grossinger's he paraphrased JFK's inau-
gural address. He's living in the past."

Two little-publicized episodes will, I think, shed some useful
light on the real Sorensen who has lived for years behind the
protective mythology of Camelot. One concerns Sorensen's con-

duct at the tumultuous 1968 Democratic convention, and the other centers on the book he published last year called *The Kennedy Legacy*.

During the Chicago convention, I had a few drinks with Paul Gorman, a speechwriter for Eugene McCarthy. Gorman angrily told me Sorensen was "trying to double-cross the peace people" through some complicated and devious maneuvers over the drafting of the minority antiwar, anti-LBJ plank for the platform. But my mind was on the violent streets, and I didn't really follow Gorman's intricate tale of betrayal. A few months later it completely left my mind.

But I recently came into possession of a private memorandum drafted by author and presidential adviser Richard Goodwin that chronicles in Byzantine detail Sorensen's double game at the 1968 convention. Because of its importance, and in the vagrant hope the daily press will pick it up, I quote from Goodwin's memo, dated September 10, 1968, at some length.

"I arrived in Chicago the evening of Thursday, August 22, and was greeted with the following appalling news: the doves on the platform committee—about thirty-five people including some who were obviously not doves—had set up a separate group. There were five or six McCarthy delegates on this committee, one McGovern man, and the rest were 'uncommitted,' including Ted Sorensen. The drafting committee met and [John] Gilligan said, 'I don't know who should be chairman of this meeting. I suppose you've had the most experience, Ted. You do it.' Ted modestly accepted, and pointed out that a group can't write a platform, so he will parcel out assignments, and they can all meet tomorrow to consider the drafts. He asks a professor—one of our delegates —to write something about Czechoslovakia, [William] Clark to write a preamble about how bad the war is, someone else to do 'no more Vietnams,' and then he says, 'And I'll do the Vietnam plank.' Everyone nods and it is decided. The McCarthy delegates at this meeting are fine, intelligent people but with almost no political sophistication at all. They really believe everyone there is solely motivated by the desire to end the war in Vietnam.

"When I heard this I practically fell out of my chair. The whole charade had clearly been prearranged in order to take the peace issue away from the two candidates for President who represented that issue, and even prevent the issue from ever reaching the floor. I called Frank Mankiewicz in Washington, who was working for McGovern, I told him the facts and asked him what he thought was happening. 'I know goddam well what's happening,' he said. 'They're trying to steal the peace issue.' We agreed the only way to counter was to draft a peace plank that was agreed to by both McCarthy and McGovern, and present that agreed draft to the informal 'dove' committee when they reconvened to consider the Sorensen draft. Frank suggested I call [Pierre] Salinger who was in Chicago to work for McGovern. I told Pierre what had gone on. His only comment was 'Sorensen is screwing'. . . .

"Friday morning the draft was read over the phone to McCarthy and McGovern. We gave it to Shields [Gilligan's campaign manager in Ohio] thinking Gilligan would present it as the agreed-upon position of the mayor candidates. That should take care of the Sorensen effort, which ostensibly only represented his personal views. But I was still uneasy, called Salinger, and said, 'Those guys might pull anything, we better go to that meeting.' We drove to the Stockyards Inn and entered the meeting room. We came as representatives of McGovern and McCarthy and were both delegates to the convention. As soon as Sorensen saw us, he had us thrown out on the grounds that we were not on his committee, which, of course, was itself a purely informal and ad hoc group.

"We spent the day sitting around the Stockyards Inn, talking to reporters and having our delegates come out and report to us periodically. No sooner had we left [the meeting] than the McCarthy-McGovern draft was pocketed—not even shown to the committee—and the Sorensen draft was placed on the table. We asked for a copy of the draft and were refused. But our delegates came out and told us the substance of the proposals. They consisted of the administration position, stated more gently and with slightly more ambiguity than Dean Rusk, although there was no substantive proposal that Rusk could not agree with. Pierre then started to brief the press intensively—telling them that the whole committee ploy was an effort to destroy the peace forces on behalf of Humphrey. He was brutal—and it was true. . . .

"Finally, at about 3 P.M., we got them [the McCarthy delegates] to protest our exclusion. There was a vote and we were allowed in just as the Sorensen draft was being retyped to reflect the day's debate. Ted handed it over silently as we came in. The preamble was strong and good—written by Clark—and my first reaction was maybe we won't have a clash at all. But as I continued reading, it was clear that it was the administration position all over again. The bombing halt required a quid pro quo, and even worse, any American withdrawal of forces was conditioned on a cease fire. In other words, we wouldn't take out any troops until the war was over. . . . Not only did the draft cut the heart out of the peace position, but it destroyed the proposal for withdrawal which Ted Kennedy had just made. . . . And Sorensen had worked on that speech. . . .

"Of course, in retrospect, we know LBJ wasn't going to let Humphrey even sound different on Vietnam. He wanted a complete vindication of his policies, which he got. But Humphrey did want a plank of his own, and one that would isolate the McCarthy and McGovern forces, making them appear like extremists or rigid ideologues. In this effort, Sorensen was Humphrey's agent, while asserting his independence, and even his fidelity to the completely different policies of Robert Kennedy. . . ."

Then there is the matter of Sorensen's book *The Kennedy Legacy*. *The New York Times* originally invited me to review this book. I read it in galleys and was so disgusted I called the *Times* and told them I didn't want to write the review because the book was boring and worthless, and I was reluctant to say so because I had just published my own Kennedy book and feared people would attribute my hostility to competitive instincts.

But now that Sorensen has been nominated for the United States Senate, I feel free to make a few comments about the book.

Sorensen, after advising Ted Kennedy about Chappaquiddick, after ghosting his television speech, then—at great expense to his publisher—changed the galleys of his book to edit out favorable references to Kennedy when the Senator's popularity began to plummet.

In the galleys I read for the *Times*, Sorensen quoted a telephone conversation he had with Ted Kennedy during the 1968 convention: "As certain as anything could be certain in politics, I told Ted, he was young enough to have more and even better opportunities for the presidency in the future."

That quote does not appear in the book.

In the galleys, Sorensen concluded a long section on youth and students with a quotation from Ted Kennedy: "As Senator Edward Kennedy has stated. . . ."

That innocuous quote, too, mysteriously vanished after Chappaquiddick.

In the galleys, Sorensen criticized Eugene McCarthy because of "his vote against Ted Kennedy for Senate whip." Sorensen changed the sentence to read because of "his vote for Russell Long for Senate whip." That was the only change in the paragraph.

The mythology of Ted Sorensen as a Kennedy liberal still endures in many places—largely because journalists are so conformist and lazy it usually takes years for a politician's reputation to catch up with his reality.

I don't know when Sorensen began to turn sour. Some people who know him say he never was very humane or courageous. Others say it was the trauma of Dallas that made him cynical and self-centered.

But the lesson is that no man can spend a lifetime working in the orbit of a family like the Kennedys and retain sure sense of who he really is.

Sorensen might have spent the years since Dallas differently. He might have spent time in Bed-Stuy, or in the Mississippi Delta, or in Appalachia, learning from the same raw experiences that transformed Robert Kennedy. He might have worked for Ralph Nader instead of General Motors. He might have gone to the campuses to listen, instead of just picking up lecture fees for his campaign chest. He might have renewed his humanist reflexes by joining a cause, helping the Vietnam Moratorium like Galbraith and Dutton, working with the McCarthy kids in New Hampshire like Goodwin, improving a newspaper like Bill Moyers, becoming a witness for the Chicago Conspiracy like Ramsey Clark.

But Sorensen just served corporation clients, played politics, took no unpopular positions, gave bad advice to the Kennedys—and became a burnt-out case.

April 30, 1970

BILL MOYERS DAZZLES GRADUALLY

Television news is a corporate, conformist, and committee enterprise. The illusion of objectivity and the avoidance of controversy are prized. Diversity and individuality are unappreciated. The governing assumption is that the audience has a ninety-second attention span. Usually, it is a kingdom where the bland lead the blind.

Network news anchors are selected by a mysterious alchemy that measures how reassuring their personality is. Power groupies like Barbara ("Be kind to us, Mr. President") Walters are presented as giants of journalism. Positioning camera crews outside the homes of Wayne Williams or Richard Allen is considered investigative reporting.

Documentaries of distinction are infrequent. Most of them present facts without meaning. When a program of meaty substance does get on the air—like CBS's series on national defense —it unsettles the whole industry.

But now, this corporate formula, this conformist mold, is being broken. Bill Moyers is stretching the rules. Ideas, a civic passion, a point of view, and a rich, complicated, *individual* sensibility are on the CBS network several times each week, piercing the bland glacier of commercial television, entering the twenty million American minds through the awesome medium that Moyers himself calls "the campfire of modern America."

Moyers knows something that no one else in television news seems to comprehend. As he puts it: "Most of the news on television is, unfortunately, whatever the government says is news. It's our job to inform people what really is going on."

What makes Moyers' return to CBS so potentially significant is the immense trust he seems to have with ordinary citizens. Moyers authentically possesses the American values and symbolism that Jimmy Carter tried to package and retail.

Moyers really is a religious, Southern, small-town populist. The son of an Oklahoma sharecropper, he grew up in tiny Marshall, Texas, "where the streets are named after Jim Bowie and Sam Houston."

Moyers does have a religious faith. He is an ordained Baptist minister who remains preoccupied with theological questions about the purpose of life and the meaning of morality.

His streak of populism runs deep. And it is a profoundly democratic, antiracist populism. To Moyers, the legal principle of one man, one vote "is the bible" and he sees big political money as the intruder that corrupts the purity of one man, one vote.

Audience surveys and other tests have found that Moyers has a devoted following among younger liberals, but also among his own kin—rural, Southern, fundamentalist conservatives. Last year, the Christian Alert, a right-wing watchdog group, cited "Bill Moyers Journal" on the Public Broadcasting System as the only television program it did not find objectionable—even though the "Journal" had a stunning segment which exposed the manipulation and bigotry of the evangelical "demagogues."

It is this catholic constituency, touched by Moyers through America's campfire, that tingles the imagination.

But it also creates an element of risk, tension, and even high drama. By most accounts, including David Halberstam's *The Powers That Be*, CBS television is a particularly Darwinian environment, littered with the corpses of losers in office politics. And unlike newspapers, television is licensed by the federal government. This leads political insiders, media insiders, a lot of plain citizens—and Moyers himself—to wonder just how long he can survive with complete freedom at CBS if the economy worsens and the right-wing starts hunting for diversionary scapegoats.

Although the "CBS Evening News" has rotating sponsorship, what happens if one corporation tries to organize an advertising boycott of CBS because of Moyers? What happens if the ratings dip and some self-censoring executive starts cutting Moyers' segments in half? What happens if Senator Helms or Senator Denton makes a speech claiming that Moyers is using his position at CBS to run for President in 1984?

But there are also strong circumstances operating in protection of the Moyers experiment. He was rehired by CBS three months ago because the boss—Chairman of the Board William Paley—wanted him rehired. Since Moyers' return, the ratings have been going up. The CBS network "Evening News" is now one full rating point ahead of NBC and ABC—in a ratings war, where fractions of a point have economic significance. A full-

rating point advantage on the nightly news translates i͏
tional advertising revenue of about $7 million over a ye͏
Gordon Sauter, the new president of CBS News, has be͏
portive of Moyers. And so has Dan Rather, who might ha͏ ͏ ͏elt
threatened or envious.

And Bill Moyers himself does not make an easy target for the hard right. His philosophy is neither static nor predictable. He is a self-described "cultural conservative." (So am I.) He is skeptical of bureaucracy and big government. He has repeatedly pointed out the intellectual bankruptcy of the current Democratic party and has a sharp eye for the mushy cliches of liberalism. And like Robert Coles and Paul Cowan, Moyers has the ability to convey, with empathy and respect, the views of people he does not agree with.

Moyers is also a brilliant politician. His friend of twenty years, Bill Haddad, says: "Bill understands power and the limits of power completely. He has an instinct for knowing just how far he can go, without losing what he already has."

Moyers himself likes to quote Emily Dickinson: "Truth must dazzle gradually—lest it blind."

In this society, breaking away to tell a deeper truth is problematic. You might lose, like Curt Flood, or Frank Serpico, or George McGovern. Or you might become a liberating legend, like Jackie Robinson, or Judge Frank Johnson, or Edward R. Murrow.

On December 8, 1981, Bill Moyers was on the CBS network news for exactly five minutes and twenty-six seconds. He did an exposé of the vast money and power behind a gigantic consumer fraud being pulled by the Northwest Alaskan Pipeline Company. That week the Congress was set to approve legislation that required natural-gas consumers to pay, in advance, through their monthly bills, the refinancing of the billion project because the banks would not underwrite refinancing of the venture. The Moyers segment detailed how the natural-gas pipeline consortium had hired: the law firm of Democratic party National Chairman Charles Manatt; the law firm of former Democratic Chairman Robert Strauss; former Vice-President Walter Mondale as a "consultant"; the law firm of Lee White, former chairman of the Federal Power Commission under Lyndon Johnson; and the pub-

lic relations firm of Peter Hannaford, who had purchased the
consulting firm owned by Richard Allen, and is the former business partner of Reagan aide Michael Deaver. As icing to all this
influence, John McMillian, the president of the pipeline company, made $80,000 in political contributions since he won the
pipeline contract. Moyers ran a "visual crawl" listing all these
donations across the television screen.

And Moyers, who is a master of political symbolism, presented
as costars of his segment two balanced ideological bookends:
conservative Republican Congressman Tom Corcoran of Illinois
and liberal Democratic Senator Howard Metzenbaum of Ohio.

He displayed Corcoran saying: "Here we have potentially the
greatest consumer rip-off in the history of the United States—$37
billion," and observing that the Democrats "took a walk on this
one, probably for political reasons."

And he displayed Metzenbaum saying: "Not long ago, one of
my staffers called a staffer for another senator and said, 'Is your
senator going to be with us on this issue?' And the response was,
'Oh no, he couldn't be with you. He took a lot of money from
the oil companies during his campaign.' Now that actually happened."

I had never seen anything so powerful on a nightly network
news show. Moyers had somehow synthesized diverse television
techniques—commentary, computer-generated graphics, subtle
documentary-style camera work, to make unforgettable a "non-
visual" story. Moyers ended the story by telling twenty million
countrymen: "The two-party system is not only up for grabs—it's
up for sale." Hardly the polite irony of Brinkley, or the Olympian
detachment of Severeid.

Dan Rather, who functions as the managing editor of the
nightly news as well as the anchorman, made the decision to give
Moyers the unusually long time to tell the pipeline story. The
director and executive producer of the network news first saw the
story ten minutes before it went on the air; the president of CBS
News and other corporate executives saw it for the first time on
the air. The very first call Moyers received after the piece aired
on the 6:30 feed was from Van Gordon Sauter. Sauter reached
Moyers in his office and told him the piece was great and that it
didn't seem five minutes long—perhaps the highest compliment

from the man responsible for the news division's ratings and profits.

Ralph Nader, our unfashionable national treasure, gave Moyers the original nudge to do the pipeline piece. Nader watched the segment with his staff in his office, and told me; "It was like a thunderbolt. It left people gasping. It had an unbelievable impact in Washington. Mondale may never recover."

Nader also offers an insight into one facet of Moyers' versatile talent. The enormity of the pipeline's consumer injury had been bugging Nader for months. Nader really understands energy industry financing, and he had tried repeatedly to stimulate print interest in this theft from the common man.

"But it was too arcane, too abstract, too technical for most reporters," he says. "The *Wall Street Journal* wouldn't cover it but ran an editorial endorsing the waiver legislation. The wire services did bits and pieces, but the story required an intelligent overview to give it meaning." (Part of Nader's equally versatile talent is that he functions as a pro bono assignment editor and fact checker for at least twenty-five journalists.)

"Finally, a week before the final vote, I called Moyers," Nader recalls. "He understood it *instantly*. He reacted differently than everyone else I talked to."

Moyers, of course, grew up in Texas politics and worked for Lyndon Johnson, and knows in his blood, from autobiographical knowledge, how the oil and gas interests have bought favors in Washington for generations.

Moyers and his producer Martin Koughan put the pieces together in seven days, with Koughan working all weekend.

"It would have been a two-parter, if we only had time," Koughan laments.

Although the pipeline waiver passed the House on December 10 by 230 to 188, five and a half minutes of Moyers on the network did change about fifty votes and caused a tremendous backlash within the defensive Congress—an institution with a higher per capita crime rate in the last session than the 41st precinct in the South Bronx.

Congressman Young of Alaska attacked Moyers on the floor of the House on December 9. He said: "It is unfortunate there have been many misnomers pronounced on this floor, and especially by CBS News last night, Mr. Moyers's program. If you think there is freedom of the press in the United States, I want to tell you there is no freedom of the press. They print one side of the issue, never contact anybody else on the other side, never tried to participate, as far as the Ralph Nader group goes, in the hearings to give some alternatives, ideas, suggestions. Then they come out with the cheap shot. The press should be ashamed of itself. . . ."

And Jim Wright of Texas, the Democratic Majority Leader of the House of Representatives, wrote a letter of complaint. But he did not write to Bill Moyers, whom he has known for twenty years. He wrote to Bill Leonard, the president of CBS News. Wright ended his letter this way: "It is one thing to provide your listeners with intelligent and informed comment; it is quite another to sanction the kind of hatchet job exemplified by Mr. Moyers commentary of Tuesday evening. I urge that you reread or replay his commentary, and then ask yourself whether this is consistent with the integrity you strive for in CBS News."

On the other hand, Moyers carefully maintains a thick folder of letters from ordinary viewers who were moved by the pipeline segment to write to him. He hoards these letters the way a shrewd politician keeps a file of all the constituents he has helped with Social Security and Veterans' benefits.

From Blairstown, New Jersey: "My wife and I simply cannot think of words strong enough to congratulate you on last night's report of the Alaska pipeline rip-off."

From a professor in the religion department of Wichita State University in Kansas: "I had wondered whether you would be able to continue such unvarnished reporting and analysis at CBS, and I can't say how pleased I am that so far you have been able to. With cooptation on the left and sellout on the right, unbiased but trenchant analysis is a rare entity indeed."

From a woman in Cuyahoga Falls, Ohio: "You were simply great Tuesday night on the McMillian deal. Perhaps the whole situation is hopeless as long as money has the loudest voice, but if no one lets us in on what chicanery goes on, then it is certainly hopeless. I am sending notes to both Mr. Leonard and Mr. Benjamin for having the courage to let you tell the truth. I have a hunch you had to insist. . . ."

And Ralph Nader thinks the pipeline segment will have a lasting impact on the politicians. He says: "The pipeline corporation is going to come back to Congress next year for long guarantees. They probably won't get away with that one because of what Moyers did."

In 1960, Bill Moyers was teaching theology at Baylor University in Waco, Texas, when Lyndon Johnson summoned him for his presidential campaign. Moyers would become Johnson's surrogate son, living in his home for a few months in 1961; flying back with him on Air Force One from Dallas in 1963; functioning as his principal assistant on shaping domestic policy; and managing his election campaign against Barry Goldwater in 1964. At age twenty-eight, Bill Moyers was helping to write the populist laws of the Great Society. During this period Tom Wicker wrote a profile of Moyers in *Harper's* magazine called "Johnson's Good Angel."

But Bill Moyers was not a hawk on Vietnam, and he was not a sychophant. So his deep friendship with the president of the United States began to disintegrate with the escalation of the Vietnam war during the second half of 1965. Johnson made him press secretary, to defend in public a war whose purposes Moyers doubted in private—and this further strained the relationship. In 1974, James Fallows wrote a tough-minded, perceptive profile of Moyers—that was critical of his inner need for an establishment "Daddy." Fallows' *Washington Monthly* article described how Moyers sought to escape as press secretary and replace George Ball as undersecretary of state in 1966:

"The odds were all against him [Moyers]. The symbolic demands of international diplomacy required that blue-bloods fill the position; Moyers's abilities were not enough to offset his North Texas State Teachers College background. But such were his efforts that when it came time to fill the position, Johnson had to bring in invincible armor—Nicholas DeB. Katzenbach, Princeton, Oxford, Yale, upper-crust—to hold Moyers out."

In the end, it was a death in the family that finally compelled Moyers to leave Lyndon Johnson. Moyers' older brother James committed suicide in September of 1966, and Moyers took responsibility for the financial support of his brother's widow and her two daughters. He had to find a larger income than the White

House offered. And by then Moyers' influence had dwindled; Rostow and Bundy were in the saddle, expanding the war in Vietnam; and Moyers had developed health problems from all the tension.

The final parting between Moyers and LBJ was agonizing; the two men never reconciled. In his bitter exile, Johnson bad-mouthed Moyers as an ungrateful defector to the Kennedys. But Moyers, for his part, kept rejecting big-money offers to write "the inside story" of the Johnson presidency. Moyers' friends say he was overjoyed when he received a letter from Lady Bird Johnson in 1980, congratulating him for his show on the evangelical right.

Bill Moyers gravitated toward another mentor in 1967—the eccentric Captain Harry Guggenheim, who hired him as publisher of *Newsday*. They were an odd couple. The crochety Guggenheim admired Richard Nixon and favored a military victory in Vietnam, while Moyers was becoming more and more convinced the war was a mistake. At the same time, Moyers was publicly being groomed to take over the paper from the elderly proprietor.

Moyers did a fine job as publisher of *Newsday;* he sent Saul Bellow to cover the Six-Day war, he gave Pete Hamill a column, and the paper won two Pulitzers during his three years in the job. One was for a lengthy investigative series exposing the grubby Republican politicians who ran Nassau County. But some of those same local Republican bosses—including William Casey— were cronies of Guggenheim, and they gradually persuaded the owner that Moyers was a radical who had hired a bunch of left-wing editors.

Guggenheim suffered a stroke in 1969 and knew he was dying of cancer. He demanded that Moyers purge the staff of "left-wing reporters," and of one editor who Guggenheim said was "a communist." Moyers refused and Guggenheim sold the paper out from under him, to the Los Angeles Times-Mirror Corporation. A condition of the sale, reportedly, was the termination of Moyers as publisher. At the final hour, Moyers himself made a better offer to purchase the paper for $5 million more, but Guggenheim sold it, for the lesser amount, to the solid, conservative Times-Mirror.

This was the second traumatic separation for Moyers in four

years. This one took time to heal. His friend Willie Morris, then editor of *Harper's*, assigned him to journey across the country, talking to average people, listening to their stories. This project became Moyers' only book—*Listening to America*—which Anthony Lewis called "beautiful, marvelous."

It was only after two painful disappointments that Bill Moyers, at age thirty-seven, began his third career in 1971. He chose to become a television journalist. In his third career, he would break his dependency on mentors, find himself, invent his own independence, and continue to grow in a way that reminds me of how Robert Kennedy grew in public, later in his life, after great disappointment. A difference is that Kennedy grew *with* his times, and Moyers grew *against* his.

The great paradox is that Bill Moyers can't stand being interviewed. The man who is so skillful at putting others at ease and gently drawing them out, who is so good at asking informed, inviting questions and then listening, will do almost anything to avoid analyzing himself. Or reading an analysis of Bill Moyers by someone else.

A friend suggests that Moyers is an "anguished soul" who is "harder on himself than any critic can possibly be. He knows how superficial any article must be, compared to what he has already thought about himself. . . . He has all kinds of guilts and doubts, but hides them and works twenty hours a day."

Last October Ann Crittenden—another Texan—published an excellent profile of Moyers in *Channels* magazine. But Moyers hated it, because it probed his psyche too speculatively and, he says, reported gossip as historical fact.

Moyers first tried to talk Crittenden out of doing the piece, then broke one interview appointment in New York. Finally Crittenden had to fly out to Aspen, Colorado, to pin him down.

Then, before the article was published, Moyers sent Crittenden an extraordinary nineteen-page, handwritten letter. It was beautifully written, and attempted to explain himself on his own terms and perhaps to preempt or control an article he did not want.

The letter was so good *Channels* published excerpts from it as a sidebar to the Crittenden profile.

In two poetic, autobiographical passages, Moyers wrote to

Crittenden: "Having been propelled as a young man into a conspicuous place and having moved on to a base in New York, I was easy pickin's for the Establishment. There was the temptation, and I went on the board of the Rockefeller Foundation, became a trustee of the Council of Foreign Affairs (in each case the youngest), got invited to Bilderberg, etc. But some old instinct prevailed, and the crucial decision came in the very early seventies when David Rockefeller and his committee, searching for the first full-time president of the Council on Foreign Relations, offered me the job—with an apartment on Park Avenue and all that. . . . I declined. I declined because I had begun to find in television a joy—yes, joy—incompatible with power and prestige. And I had begun to realize that in journalism lay the route to independence. For if a man has a skill he can take with his tent, he need never be fearful of obeying his heart."

And this, on the last of the nineteen pages: "It is past midnight and I have rambled on, less eager I suppose, to fill in the blanks than, by showing you how difficult it is to fill them in, to stay you from even continuing your effort. I am always—almost always—reluctant to talk openly about myself, and even more so in this transition. The future is never the past, and I would rather have the work I have done analyzed than myself. . . ."

Bill Moyers began his prime during the last two years at PBS, even as PBS was abandoning public affairs and shrinking his production budget, forcing him to do more studio-based interview shows without his extended family of independent producers, like Sherry Jones in Washington and Mark and Lisa Benjamin in New York. (Moyers' favorite producer, the radical Al Levin, was on the staff of the "Journal.")

Working against weekly deadlines, Moyers produced one show after another that established new standards for excellence in television, the way his hero Ed Murrow did during the 1950s.

Some of the interviews were memorable for their intellectual chemistry and historical instruction. My personal favorite was a two-parter with his fellow southerner, former federal judge Frank Johnson, who wrote all the landmark Court decisions on school integration and voting rights in Alabama during the 1950s and 1960s, in defiance of popular prejudice and racist Governor George Wallace.

Moyers also did a series of wonderful conversations with senior wise men and women of the human tribe: cultural critic George Steiner; novelist and poet Robert Penn Warren; writer Dame Rebecca West; and myth-explorer Joseph Campbell. These shows helped illuminate how much enthusiasm, awe, and humility Moyers retains as a perpetual pupil of the heavyweights.

Moyers also created three astonishing documentary essays during this growth spurt: the evangelical movement on September 26, 1980, provided by Martin Koughan; a prophetic warning against the economic peril of ever-larger military expenditures, produced by Al Levin, on May 8, 1981, and a compelling defense of women's right to abortion on May 15, 1981, produced by Randy Bean.

All of Moyers' versatile talents converged on these three shows. The ability to translate abstract concepts into emotions and images. The sixth sense that anticipates the timely subject. And the intellect that thinks systemically.

The evangelical show was taped at a convention of 15,000 fundamentalist Christians meeting in Dallas. With curiosity and a sense of fairness, Moyers interviewed the people attending this right-wing revival meeting. He did not ridicule or caricature them. He gave them their full say on camera.

And then, at the end of the hour, Moyers delivered his own sermon. Standing in the eye of America's campfire, Moyers cut to the essence of it all:

I know the people in this report. I was born and reared among them: they're my kin. Although long ago I made passage to another place and culture, to another way of seeing and believing, I still hear at certain times and with affection echoes of their prayers and hymns. I recognize deeply imprinted within me the inherited yearning for order and authority that caused them in menacing times to cleave more tenaciously to their faith.

It isn't surprising that they're fighting back against the discoveries of science, decrees of government, and dilemmas of democracy that intrude upon their fixed scheme of things. Nor is it unprecedented for people of a religious persuasion to want to affect the system, to matter politically, to try to elect to office agents of their anger who will attempt to supply the leadership for which they ache. There are precedents aplenty. I once wrote a speech for Lyndon Johnson asking Southern Baptists to rally behind the Voting Rights Act of 1965. A Catholic bishop urges his parishioners to vote for candidates who oppose abortion. Jimmy Carter prowls black churches as if they were precincts of the Democratic party, which many are. William Sloane Coffin marshals his congregation to march on the Pentagon, and Jews pressure Washington to support Israeli government decisions based on interpretations of scriptures from the Bronze Age, precedents all.

It is not that the evangelicals are taking politics seriously that bothers me. It's the lie they're being told by the demagogues who flatter them into believing they can achieve politically the certitude they have embraced theologically. The world doesn't work that way. There is no heaven on earth. Nor can our democracy agree to a moral majority that makes religious doctrine the test of political opinion. You may have that only where all are alike in thought and root and intent, which America is not. Here, the idea has long been to protect religious freedom from a carnivorous state, political deliberation from dogmatic zealots, and militant believers from one another.

So they're being misled, these people, by manipulators of politics masquerading as messengers of heaven, and their hearts will be broken by false gods who, having taken the coin of their vote or purse, will move on to work the next crowd. The same Reverend Falwell who claims a divine mandate to go right into the halls of Congress and fight for laws that will save America is caught lying in public about a meeting he had with the President. Ronald Reagan, having endorsed the Moral Majority in Dallas, moves on to a luncheon given for him by teamsters in Ohio whose chieftains include four men either indicted or convicted or being investigated for corrupt practices. Some majority. Some morality.

Why did Bill Moyers quit public television to return to commercial television?

It is a question he agonized over for more than a year. He negotiated, in a semipublic fashion, with all three networks, before settling on CBS even though ABC offered him more money and perks.

There are many motives why, at the beginning of his prime, Moyers left public television. A larger audience, bigger budgets, access to more advanced technology, vast resources, and greater personal freedom, all contributed to the final decision.

Moyers understood, probably better than anyone else in the whole country, how tragically and irrevocably the promise of public television has been annulled.

Moyers, along with Alex Haley, John Gardner, and thirteen other wise citizens, was a member of the Carnegie Commission that composed a landmark study, called *A Public Trust*, on the future of public broadcasting. This document concluded: "We find public broadcasting's financial, organizational, and creative structure fundamentally flawed.

"In retrospect, what public broadcasting tried to invent was a truly radical idea; an instrument of mass communication that simultaneously respects the artistry of individuals who create programs, the needs of the public that form the audience, and the forces of political power that supply the resources.

"Sadly, we conclude that the invention did not work. . . ."

By the late 1970s, corporate underwriting began to determine programming on PBS. Public affairs and local news were dropped, and arts programs and subsidized conservatives like Milton Friedman and William Buckley got on the air, along with "Wall Street Week."

In 1980 and 1981, the budget for "Bill Moyers' Journal" was cut 25 percent—50 percent if adjusted for inflation. "Journal" producer Al Levin says: "The whole decision-making process of PBS was driving Bill crazy. There was no uniform air time for the show across the country. Local affiliates had the power, not the PBS network. Local affiliates had the power to preempt a show, or air it at three in the afternoon, if they wanted, without any promotion. . . . In every city, the local affiliate station is run by the local elite."

Another factor was that the only corporate underwriter of "Bill Moyers' Journal" pulled out in 1980. The Weyerhaeuser Corporation—a paper products and chemicals conglomerate—supplied about 20 percent of the funding for the "Journal." Early in 1980, the "Journal" did shows on Barry Commoner, Big Business Day, and the congressional attempt to abolish the regulatory function of the FTC. All three shows had a strong anticorporate thrust. And although Moyers himself typically will not talk about it, his staff is convinced that these three editions of the "Journal" caused the cancellations of corporate underwriting by the Weyerhaeuser Corporation.

According to Martin Koughan: "When we lost Weyerhaeuser, it meant we had no money for producing shows in the field. It took the visual dimension out of the "Journal." It cut us off from all those young, independent producers Bill loved to cooperate with."

Bill Moyers is not anybody's "good angel." He is a complicated, driven, private man. He is not a genius, or even an original thinker like Campbell, Steiner, or Saul Bellow.

But at this hour in history, he is one of a kind. He is an investigative moralist with a franchise to appear on network television whenever he has something to say. Just by doing that, he is filling a void in Ronald Reagan's supply-side America.

Bill Moyers is not some lonely hero infiltrating a giant institution. There are important CBS decision makers who have consciously awarded Moyers this franchise because they have faith in his talent. The best producers, cameramen, tape editors, artists, researchers, and computer technology have been put at his disposal by CBS. Dan Rather has staked his future as Cronkite's successor on this Moyers experiment in quality.

But at the same time, there are concentrations of power, in the corporations, in the Congress, who fear Moyers and wish to do him harm. They understand that Bill Moyers is attempting something profound. He is breaking away from the mass media's historic role—in Al Levin's phrase—"of validating the system."

All three television networks are now planning to expand their nightly network news broadcasts to a full hour, either this fall or in 1983. They are taking this step because news makes money for the television corporations. More Americans—about sixty million —watch the news each night on CBS, NBC, and ABC, than watch the prime-time programming that comes on after 8 P.M. The "Evening News" creates more advertising revenue for CBS than "Dallas" or "The Dukes of Hazzard." In 1981, the "CBS Evening News" generated about *one hundred million dollars* in revenues.

If the Moyers experiment does well in the marketplace, like "60 Minutes," if its ratings continue to be strong, it will evolutionize television journalism. It will make TV journalism finally grow up. It will make contagious good writing, in-depth muckraking, individual sensibility, boat-rocking commentary—and skepticism about government definitions of what news is.

The other copycat commercial networks, in order to fill the coming hour of news, will go out and find investigative moralists in the Moyers mold, instead of the old mold Moyers is trying to break. Imagine Sy Hersh using those computer-generated graphics to expose the CIA on the NBC network news. Imagine Roger Wilkins or Felipe Luciano producing visual essays that reach twenty million people on ABC's "World News Tonight."

But if this experiment to create new forms of television journalism should fail, if this test of corporate freedom should end badly, then Bill Moyers, who has acquired self-knowledge and independence, will know what to do. As he has already written:

"For if a man has a skill he can take with his tent, he need never be fearful of obeying his heart."

January 26, 1982

6

Obituaries for
Two Millionaires

Nelson Rockefeller and Robert Kennedy were both rich kids who wanted to be president. Rockefeller was the governor of New York and Kennedy was the U.S. senator from New York. But there the similarities stop.

These are the two obits I wrote the week each one died. The Rockefeller obituary was composed in reaction to the platitudinous eulogies that washed away all his sins in life. My piece tried to restore a realistic perspective to a powerful politician's public career. It did not deal with the titillating circumstances of his death, which others dwelled on, because I have never written about anyone's private life, and I hope I never will. It dealt with the central themes and actions of his public life.

I loved Robert Kennedy, and his obituary was written in one twelve-hour cathartic sitting the day after his funeral. I am writing now fifteen years after his murder, and his loss hurts even more with the passage of time, because I understand better now how unique and irreplaceable he was.

We can now, I think, say of Robert Kennedy, what Guy Dumur said of Albert Camus after his death: "He would have been a force in reserve, a bridge between the past and the future. He would have been one from whom we awaited a response that, when it came, would have been heard by all."

NELSON ROCKEFELLER

Unpleasant facts are the first casualty when a powerful man dies —the Cronkites and Restons recall only the decencies. In his Sunday *Times* obit for Nelson Rockefeller, James Reston wrote: "Henry Kissinger, when he learned that Rockefeller had died, recalled how he had always kept asking: 'What's the right thing to do?' "

But the truth is that even if Nelson raised such a moral question, the answer that came to him was frequently inhuman, colonial, and wrong.

On the two transcendental moral issues of our time—Vietnam and Watergate—Rockefeller blew it. When he ran in the 1964 Republican primaries, he supported the Vietnam war, urging its escalations upon Lyndon Johnson. On April 27 of that year, while campaigning in Oregon, Rockefeller said:

"Winning the fight for freedom in Vietnam is essential to the survival of freedom in all of Asia. The communist guerrillas must be defeated. . . . The administration should declare without reservation that it will withdraw no more American forces from Vietnam until the military situation justifies such action. The administration should make clear that it supports the existing government in Saigon and should cease from criticizing it."

Four years later, in the spring of 1968, Rockefeller briefly spoke like a dove as he tried to win votes on campuses and in the suburbs. But as soon as Nixon and Agnew were nominated, he easily switched again to enthusiasm for the bombing.

In October of 1969, when the madness of our policy was apparent to a majority of his countrymen and the Vietnam Moratorium was being held on campuses across the nation, Rockefeller went on television to praise Nixon's "handling of the war."

In the realm of foreign policy, Kissinger was his tutor. In 1969, Rockefeller wrote the unspeakable Latin America report for the Nixon administration, recommending support for military dictatorships on the grounds of their stability and predictability. On his fact-finding mission in preparation of that report he posed, smiling, on a balcony with the Haitian tyrant and torturer Francois Duvalier, in a tropical parody of the Hubert Humphrey–Lester Maddox embrace.

In his report he wrote: "The authoritarian and hierarchical tradition, which has conditioned and formed the cultures in most of these societies, does not lend itself to the particular kind of popular government we are used to. Few of these countries, moreover, have achieved the sufficiently advanced social and economic systems required to support a consistently democratic system. For many of these societies, therefore, the question is less one of democracy or lack of it than it is simply orderly ways of getting along."

On the everlasting shame of Watergate, Rockefeller never said a word. He put party before principle and proved his loyalty by closing his eyes. Even at the point of the Saturday Night Massacre, the sacking of Cox and the resignation of his friend Eliot Richardson as attorney general, Rockefeller could not bring himself to speak against plain and clear criminals.

In song, and in common speech, the name Rockefeller was a synonym for millionaire.

But in 1965, Nelson Rockefeller vetoed a bill that guaranteed a $1.50 minimum wage to the workers of New York state. In 1967, he slashed welfare for mothers with children to 67 cents a day. In 1969 he endorsed Richard Nixon's veto of the $19.7 billion education-appropriation bill. And in 1971, he ordered that anyone earning more than $4500 a year be cut from the Medicaid rolls.

In his extraordinary novel, V, Thomas Pynchon wrote, "Alignment with the inanimate is the mark of a Bad Guy." This could almost be the epitaph on Rockefeller's tombstone. The Albany Mall cost $2 billion. When he first announced it, Rockefeller said it would cost $250 million. He could have built sixty schools with that amount of money, two high schools in every school district in the state. Rockefeller invested $1 billion to build the World Trade Center, which destroyed thousands of blue-collar jobs and small businesses in the downtown area and depressed the midtown commercial real estate market for years. The trade center has been subsidized since with state agencies renting office space at inflated prices.

Rockefeller increased the indebtedness of New York State by *700 percent* during his tenure as governor. He borrowed the idea of moral-obligation bonds from John Mitchell and helped create the fiscal crisis with his profligate bonding. It was the collapse of

Rockefeller's pet the Urban Development Corporation (UDC) that triggered the fiscal panic of February 1975.

Attica was not an aberration, not a deviation from Rockefeller's nature. It was a natural expression of his politics, and his character. The thirty-nine people who died in that massacre were poor black and Hispanic inmates and almost-poor white correction officers, the same populist coalition that was sent to die in Vietnam.

Those men died at Attica because Rockefeller would not go to the prison to join in the negotiations. The committee of citizen negotiators, including Herman Badillo and Tom Wicker, had asked—had pleaded—for Rockefeller to come just to talk, just to show his concern by coming. The hostages gave interviews over television, begging him to come. The families of the hostages sent telegrams to Rockefeller.

Instead, Rockefeller sent in his state troopers, some screaming racist slogans, shooting wildly and indiscriminately. Thirty-nine people died needlessly because of Rockefeller's stubborn arrogance and his fear of appearing weak.

In the immediate aftermath, he blamed the whole thing on black revolutionaries and militants. A year later, the 490-page McCay Commission Report was released, which severely criticized almost every aspect of Rockefeller's conduct in relation to Attica.

Yes, Nelson Rockefeller had many fine qualities. Yes, he was a cultivated man and a patron of the arts. Yes, he suffered tragedy in the death of his son and in his failure to win the prize of the presidency. Yes, he stood up to Goldwater in 1964, and once he quit politics in 1976, he had the dignity and self-knowledge to stay out.

But, at bottom, I must say that the man's life can be summed up by his lack of respect for the poorer classes, and by his colonial concept of the underdeveloped world.

The death he supported in Vietnam and inflicted himself at Attica is his legacy.

Most bad great men did at least some things that profited mankind. Robert Moses built Jones Beach to serve the poor on hot summer days. Lyndon Johnson sponsored and signed the Civil Rights Act of 1964 and began a war against poverty. Richard

Nixon opened the door to peace with China. I can't think of one such humanistic achievement by Rockefeller.

Nelson Rockefeller always reminded me of Saul Bellow's memorable title character in *Henderson the Rain King*. Bellow's fictional creation was a middle-aged millionaire who had a ceaseless voice in his heart that kept repeating, "I want! I want!"

Rockefeller also heard a selfish inner voice. It made him act like money—inherited money, not earned money—could buy anything.

The trouble was that Rockefeller's insatiable appetite had at its core, a great ambition that was bereft of the element of the humble. And was bereft of a sense of justice.

February 5, 1979

ROBERT KENNEDY

LOS ANGELES—It was a little before midnight, a half hour before he was to be assassinated, when he reached out to grasp the workingman's hand of a $75-a-week Mexican busboy in the bowels of the Ambassador Hotel.

Robert Kennedy was holding a victory cigar in his swollen and stubby fingers, and squatting on the floor of room 511. His famous political and intellectual supporters were in the room with him. The awful little pornographers of power were there too. And so were the special people, the victims and rebels Robert Kennedy identified with. Doris Huerta of the grape strike was there, and Charles Evers, and John Lewis, who once led SNCC, and Budd Schulberg, who runs a writers' workshop in Watts. And Pete Hamill and Jimmy Breslin, two gut journalists who never went to college, but who Kennedy sensed knew more about

America than the erudite Lerners, Restons, and Wechslers.

In this last hour, Kennedy seemed the most zestful, and the most inwardly serene I had seen him since Lyndon Johnson withdrew from the race. When that happened Kennedy became troubled and confused. He had lost his enemy and his crusade, and he acted like a lost soul, even as he won in Indiana. He seemed, suddenly, to not know who he was.

Defeat in Oregon, and physical exhaustion in California, had gutted his spirit even more. On Sunday he seemed somber and withdrawn as he looked blankly out of the window of his 727 Electra campaign jet. Normally Kennedy would gossip and joke with me on a campaign trip. But on Sunday all he said was that he hoped Al Lowenstein, who was supporting McCarthy, would win his congressional primary fight on Long Island. Then he turned his worn-out face to the breathtaking landscape of California.

On Monday he was drained, and his speeches flat, and he got sick to his stomach in the middle of his final campaign speech in San Diego. The press whispered about a premonition of defeat.

But now, just before midnight, he seemed to be discovering his natural rhythm again, to finally feel liberated from gloom, fatalism, and, yes, guilt over not running earlier, and somehow betraying the young he so wanted to lead.

He had won Humphrey's native state of South Dakota, and in California the Indians, and the Mexicans and the Negroes ("my people") had given him his margin of triumph. The turnout of voters in supposedly fragmented, apathetic Watts was higher than in educated, affluent Beverly Hills. Key supporters and aides of Eugene McCarthy had told Richard Goodwin earlier in the night they might now come over to Kennedy's campaign. He had come back from defeat, and won on his own. Robert Kennedy, who was always more Boston than Camelot, once again found the two things he always needed: a cause—the dispossessed—and a clear enemy.

"I am going to chase Hubert Humphrey's ass all over America," he said. "I'm going to chase his ass into every precinct. Wherever he goes, I'm going to go."

Then he went downstairs carrying his notes for a speech that would attack war and violence.

I spent the death watch in Kennedy's hotel room, watching television, and answering the grieving and bereft phone calls from as far away as London. About twenty people spent the night there, spread out among five or six rooms on the fifth floor. Occasionally a sob or shriek came out of one of the rooms. We drank all the liquor there was, but nobody got drunk.

At about 4 A.M. Adam Walinsky called from the Hospital of the Good Samaritan to mumble that the outlook was bleak. Then a tape of a speech Kennedy gave at Berkeley attacking poverty and racism flashed on, and I finally broke down. As I wept, two crew-cut employees of the Los Angeles telephone company came into the room, and mechanically began to remove the special telephones that had been installed for the evening—direct lines to the ballroom and phones used to call South Dakota and Washington. They acted as if nothing was happening, just casually pulling the wires out of the wall, and coiling them around the phones.

In another room in the suite John Lewis, who had campaigned among the hostile, middle-class Jews in California, sat on the arm of a chair, tears in his eyes, and mumbling to himself, "Why, why, why?" John Barlow Martin, his gaunt, Modigliani-like face the color of chalk, said to no one in particular, "Bomb America. Make the Coca-Cola someplace else."

Again and again the television played the drama. Kennedy's last speech, the ballsy challenge to Humphrey, the attack on the war, the jibe at Yorty, and the last awkward victory sign with his two fingers. The moan that broke across the ballroom like a wave. Men and women weeping, praying, pounding the floor.

Blair Clark, McCarthy's campaign manager, and columnist Mary McGrory, who loved Bobby almost as much as she loved Gene, came, offered condolences, fought to hold back tears, and left, reeling like sleepwalkers.

At 5:30 A.M. I went downstairs to help pick up Ed Guthman at the hospital. Outside the Ambassador Hotel sat Charles Evers, Medgar's brother. "God, they kill our friends and they kill our leaders," he said. Outside the hospital the press and a few hippies prayed.

Guthman's face said everything. Jimmy Breslin and George Plimpton left the hospital at the same time, and their faces also said that Kennedy's brain was already dead, and only his street fighter's heart kept him technically alive.

Wednesday morning I wandered around the ugly hotel. Scavengers were stealing mementoes—campaign hats, banners, posters—from the ballroom.

Now he rests next to his brother, and feelings of rage mingle with a few random personal memories of a soulful man the world thought was ruthless.

Rage at the professional Bobby haters. Not just Joe Resnick or Drew Pearson, but all those reform Democrats and liberal columnists who made hating Bobby so respectable, and even fashionable.

Rage at politicians who now urge passage of the crime bill with its gun control clause as a "memorial" to Kennedy, even though Kennedy, in life, opposed that legislation because of its provisions for wire tapping and denial of rights to defendants.

Rage at a man like Sam Yorty, who had the Los Angeles police give a traffic ticket to the entire Kennedy motorcade last week, who began red-baiting before Kennedy's heart stopped beating, and who had crashed the funeral, and refused to leave even after being asked to by Jack English.

Rage at men like Archbishop Cooke and Eric Hoffer who say America should feel no national guilt, because the assassin was a Jordanian nationalist. Rage at those eulogizers who never mention the violence of Vietnam, Mississippi, or Texas. Rage at men who cannot face the fact that the truest symbol of America is that lonesome plane from Los Angeles that carried the widows of John Kennedy, Robert Kennedy, and Martin Luther King.

But a few memories linger too.

Kennedy quietly reading the Old Testament as a private gesture of irreverence all through the three-hour funeral mass for Cardinal Spellman. Kennedy sitting in his Manhattan apartment and reading me a poem from Emerson. Kennedy visiting a migrant worker camp near Buffalo, and walking right past the manager who held a gun, and into a rotting trailer that was a home for ten migrants. Kennedy pausing while campaigning in Brooklyn in front of a small girl with glasses and suddenly saying, "My little girl wears glasses too. And I love her very much." Kennedy visiting a hospital for retarded children in Westchester last Janu-

ary, and impulsively taking sixteen patients for a ride
cream, while doctors and aides panicked.

If I had written these things two weeks ago, the *Voice* would
have been deluged with letters calling me a whore. Now many
anecdotes fill the papers and the networks, and no one doubts
them.

When he sent a plane to take Martin Luther King's widow
to Memphis, people called it a cheap political gimmick. Two
weeks ago I described him being called out of a shower in In-
dianapolis, and quipping as he groped for the phone, "Make way
for the future leader of the Free World." I got a letter saying that
proved his arrogance.

Robert Kennedy was not a saint. He was a politician.

But anyone who rode on his funeral train last Saturday, and
looked out at the rows of wounded black faces that lined the poor
side of the tracks, knew what might have been. The stone is once
again at the bottom of the hill and we are alone.
June 13, 1968

7

Heroes and Heroines

The Student Non-Violent Coordinating Committee—SNCC—doesn't exist any more. But during the early and middle 1960s, it was the frontier of virtue in America. It was the cutting edge of the civil rights movement in the rural South. And several years before Martin Luther King gave his unforgettable April 1967 speech against the Vietnam war, SNCC leaders were making the war a moral issue.

Some of the best people I've met in my life, I met in SNCC during the 1960s: Charley Cobb; Mendy Samstein, who now teaches in a public school in East Harlem; Marshal Ganz, who spent the 1970s working for Cesar Chavez; John Lewis, who is now a city Council member in Atlanta; and Bob Moses.

The piece on Moses was written a few months after I joined the staff of the *Voice* in 1964. By 1966, an exhausted, depressed Moses had left America and was living in exile in Africa. He seemed to have fallen out of history. Those of us who knew him during the sixties exchanged rumors of his fate. He remained a cult legend to the few who had crossed his path and had seen his light. Then, about 1978, I heard that he had quietly returned and was taking a few graduate courses at Harvard. And in 1981, I read that he had received one of those grants given unsolicited by the McArthur Foundation to geniuses in various realms.

Moses will probably never seek public leadership again, because the idea of leadership itself became too problematic for him. But at one moment in history, Moses gambled his life so that rural, southern blacks could vote and live in dignity. For this, he should be known and remembered by all future generations. And someday, an American Malraux or Camus may write a great novel based on his odyssey.

My essay on Muhammad Ali has a sad coda. Ali did announce his retirement shortly after this piece, but he attempted a comeback two years later. He was a shell losing to Larry Holmes, in a makeshift arena built in a Las Vegas parking lot. Ali had become an old man before my eyes. He was flat-footed, instead of on his toes; stationary instead of in constant dancing motion; slow instead of fast; off-balance instead of in perfect equilibrium.

Today, his friends worry about Ali's slurred speech and lethargic demeanor. He has not yet adjusted to the dwindling of the media's attenton, to the depletion of his entourage, to the reduction of his life-style. The transition from sports megahero to almost ordinary life has been difficult for many; very few black athletes have been as fortunate as Bill Bradley or Joe DiMaggio. Ali should have had the self-discipline not to come back. The truth is that he and Joe Frazier ruined each other in their epic war in Manila. Neither was ever the same after their brutal encounter. Ali should have quit that night, at the zenith of his career. But only Rocky Marciano has had the self-knowledge to stop at the peak, before the skills erode, and the cheering subsides.

Nevertheless, Muhammad Ali still stands as one of the greatest heroes I have seen. He risked his career for a principle when he refused to fight in Vietnam. He was stripped of his title without due process, and he was robbed of his prime—the years between twenty-six and twenty-nine, when he could not fight. Ali was a symbol of black independence; he was his own man. His good looks, wit, and intelligence broke the stereotype of the mumbling, stupid, and submissive fighter.

And on those memorable nights when Ali knocked out Sonny Liston, Cleveland Williams, George Forman, and Joe Frazier, I think he could have beaten any heavyweight who ever lived.

But I also must confess, that by the time of their third fight, I was half-rooting for Joe Frazier in my secret heart. I had psychologically come to identify more with Frazier than with Ali. To me, Ali was the soloist of genius. Frazier was the honest workman. Frazier had lightly less magical skill, but compensated for that with unquenchable will, pride, courage, and persistence. I came to think that my own limits and strengths as a journalist were more like Frazier's than Ali's.

Marcy Benstock remains as steady as the sun. She has spent the last ten years of her life trying to stop Westway—a $4 billion highway/real estate boondoggle in Manhattan. I wrote my profile/appreciation of her in 1981, and she remains a masterpiece of persistence. She still works every day to kill the highway, a contemporary female Ahab dueling the white whale of the highway lobby.

"Debts to Declare, Teachers to Thank" was a speech I gave at a roast in my honor, sponsored by the Democratic Socialists of America (DSA). It summarizes my affection for Robert Kennedy, I. F. Stone, and Murray Kempton in a fashion I don't think I can ever improve upon.

The essay on my journalistic ancestors was prompted by my frustration with a misconception of who I was. I kept getting described in articles as a "new journalist," and getting lumped together with Tom Wolfe, Eldridge Cleaver, and others I felt no particular bond with.

So I decided to write a piece (in 1972) that attempted to clear up this misunderstanding, and explain who I thought my influences were, and where my writing roots can be traced back to.

The piece pays tribute to the seminal sportswriter Jimmy Cannon, who was a great influence upon me and many other writers of my generation, especially Gay Talese and Pete Hamill. It also acknowledges another wonderful old sportswriter and novelist, W. C. Heinz, whom Jimmy Breslin calls "the best I ever saw."

I also recognize the debt I owe to naturalistic novelists like Dreiser, Dos Passos, and Nelson Algren; to oral historians like Studs Terkel and Robert Coles; and to the early 1960s journalism of Norman Mailer, which broke open a door in my mind.

This attempt at self-definition was made eleven years ago; my more mature and immediate thoughts about craft and roots are contained in the Introduction to this book. But this essay is included in this chapter as the closing piece because the quote from James Baldwin that ends the piece is still my best single credo, epitaph, and inspriation: "I want to be an honest man and a good writer."

THE INVISIBLE MAN LEARNS HIS NAME: BOB MOSES

The biblical Moses was a prophet and a liberator who drew water from a stone. For the past three years Robert Moses, also a prophet and a liberator, has been trying to draw justice from the stone of Mississippi. The difference between them is that the Old Testament Moses drew his inspiration from God and the modern Moses draws his from the housemaids, cotton pickers, and tenant farmers of Mississippi.

Robert Parris Moses, twenty-nine years old, has never met the President, he has never appeared on "Meet the Press" and he refused to be chairman of SNCC. But he is a legend among the 900,000 Negroes of Mississippi and among the sheriffs and Klansmen in that state of stone.

Driven by a philosophy that is part anarchist, part humanist, part existential, Moses quit a secure teaching job in 1961 to become SNCC's pioneer in Mississippi at $20 a week. And it was this revolutionary philosophy that drove him to defy the President and the Reverend Martin Luther King at the Democratic Convention so that the poor, uneducated Freedom Party delegates might learn to make decisions, to cleave together and return home, knowing their names, no longer invisible men, having taken their own first steps toward Canaan.

Last week Moses was in New York to receive an award from the National Guardian and to visit the parents of the murdered Mississippi volunteer, Andrew Goodman. On Wednesday, ac-

companied by his wife Donna and carrying a dog-e
Camus' *Resistance, Rebellion, and Death*, he visit
offices.

His speech is quiet, slow, poetic; his eyes sad a... ...,
manner direct yet self-effacing, not a single phrase or gesture
designed to draw attention to himself. Repeatedly during the
interview he would bring his wife into the conversation, and one
felt that he would do the same with the most illiterate Negro in
Mississippi. He sat hunched in a chair, his calloused hands
jammed into the pockets of his Navy jacket.

The beatings he suffered, the murders of his friends Medgar
Evers and Mickey Schwerner, the weeks spent in jail, the days
without sleep, the assassin's bullets that missed their mark must
have left scars, but Moses would not speak of them, perhaps
because they are too much the tokens of heroism. The first time
he was beaten in Mississippi, he threw his bloodstained shirt away
so he would not arouse the local community to violence.

"What we have found in Mississippi," he began in his anguished monotone, "is that the greatest source of strength for the
movement is the people—those poor farm hands living in chicken
coops. It is a whole series of one-to-one relationships between
SNCC workers and rural Negroes in the delta—pure and uncor-
rupted sharecroppers—that has saved the movement from turn-
ing in on itself, from becoming either abstracted or bitter. And
this nourishment from the bottom of society is something the
national leaders don't know anything about. It is these people who
must lead the movement, because they know what is needed to
make a decent life for themselves, not the national leaders who
know how to solve every problem the country faces except how
to live on $30 a week."

But Moses the antihero is the victim of an ironic paradox. The
more he withdraws to the last row at meetings, the more he
broods and introspects, the more he lives with the people who are
his sustenance, the less he says to anyone, the more his legend
grows, until it defeats his quest for equality with the most back-
ward, most brutalized partisan of the movement.

Nicholas Von Hoffman, in his new book *Mississippi Note-
book*, describes Moses as "the most trusted, the most loved of any
Southern leader."

Moses, with characteristic candor, confessed that the dinner in his honor at the Hotel Astor the night before had "depressed" him. When the audience of a thousand rose to accord him a standing ovation after a saccharine introduction, he cut it short, saying, "This is absurd. You're acting like you're part of the Establishment."

His wife, Donna, a Mississippi veteran of two years, amplified on her husband's depression. "Mississippi has nothing to do with the Old Left," she said. "The people living there need a concept of themselves, not a smug intellectual elite telling them what slogans to shout and what to do."

"The traditional left," Moses explained, "keeps talking about coalitions and leaders, but always from the top; to them Mississippi is a chess board. But it is the little people on the bottom who must learn about themselves and organize their own organizations that fulfill their own needs. . . . That's part of why I'm trying not to get alienated from these people by becoming one of those official leaders. The people don't need spokesmen or decision makers, just the confidence to try to represent themselves."

Moses believes the confrontation last August between the Freedom party and the Democratic party hierarchy in Atlantic City was "an experiment."

"The Freedom party delegates," he said, "were the only people at that whole convention who were free, who made democratic decisions. The President told all the others what to do, what to think. The others were not free in any sense of the word. Even some of the people who were sympathetic to us couldn't act on their instincts because they were so fearful they would jeopardize Humphrey's chances for the Vice-Presidency.

"When we got back to Mississippi, an old man, who was a delegate, said to me, 'I used to think Mississippi Negroes were the only people in the world who were always afraid of losing their jobs. Now I know the President of the country feels the same way.'"

The drama of August, Moses revealed, will be replayed in January, when the Freedom party, led by sharecropper Fannie Lou Hammer, challenges the seating of the entire Mississippi congressional delegation. And he suspects all the characters will portray their same old roles.

"The President will be against us," he stated, "but he will try to use us to blackmail the committee chairmen to get his legislation out of committee. The liberals will be for throwing out the racists, but not for seating us, because we're 'not legal.' Well, I say Mississippi is not legal. Their laws are illegal. We had the real election. But in the end no one will be for seating us in place of the racist congressmen because no one is willing to travel that road, because to face the truth of our claim would rip this nation apart."

Looking back, Moses believes the direction of his life was changed when he saw on television, in February 1960, a newsreel of the first student sit-in at Greensboro, North Carolina.

"Seeing that opened up a whole new world. Before that I knew nothing about the South except for, like, folk myths from a few crazy Negroes. My image of the southern Negro was fearful, cringing. But the faces on those kids were sullen, determined, and I knew this was relevant to my life."

Until February of 1960, that life consisted of a degree from Hamilton College in upstate New York, a master's degree in philosophy from Harvard in 1957, and a comfortable job teaching math at Horace Mann High School in Riverdale.

During the spring of 1960, Moses visited frequently with the nonviolent guru Bayard Rustin, and prepared to go south. During the summer he visited Amzie Moore, head of the NAACP in Cleveland, Mississippi, and the two spent a week planning a voter registration drive for the following summer. Later Moses received a letter from C. C. Bryant, the NAACP leader in McComb, suggesting his hometown as the launching pad for the drive. In July of 1961, Moses arrived alone in McComb to set in motion a chain of events whose meaning will not be clear until much more of the civil rights drama is played out.

After his three years of bruising contact with Mississippi justice and federal inertia, of living on subsistence wages in the Delta, of watching his friends be killed without retribution, I asked Moses what his "visceral feeling" to so much brutality was. He replied that the invisibility of the suffering in the national mass media was the hardest part.

"There were five murders last year before Claude Sitton wrote anything. And he is one of the best," Moses said in reference to the excellent *New York Times* reporter covering the civil rights movement.

Finally Moses began to speak of the three civil rights volunteers murdered last summer in Neshoba County while working on the summer project he directed.

"Suppose the government wasn't pretending and really wanted to indict the people who killed Andrew, James, and Mickey. Couldn't they make sure there was a grand jury that wasn't manipulated by Judge Cox? Can't they impanel a new grand jury that has some Negroes? Suppose the law is an outlaw. Suppose the sheriff is a killer and the jurors accomplices and every white man in the state a potential killer. How does a man find justice then? You tell me."

Yet despite this desperate tone, Moses has often been a decisive voice within SNCC in quelling antiwhite feeling and Mau Mau militancy, often by whites. At SNCC's 1963 convention, when there was serious talk of limiting the number of white summer volunteers, Moses argued, "Our fight is not between the black and the white but between the rational and the irrational. We must not grow up and have a racist movement. Negroes must get to know whites in all their qualities, good and bad, because that is the only way to break down the depersonalization of people."

Those close to Moses now wonder whether his current mood of bitterness and alienation has not permanently replaced his extraordinary gentleness and intellectuality. A CORE activist who admires Moses "beyond all others" reluctantly concedes that his friend, who once talked only of "the Movement," last summer began to make "petty distinctions" between SNCC, CORE, and the NAACP. Another Mississippi veteran believes the three murders and the events at the Democratic convention drove Moses toward the most intransigent elements in SNCC. But he added, "No one, black or white, can endure what Bob has without becoming as least as bitter as he. That is the nature of Mississippi."

This week Moses and his wife, bereft of imposing titles or bloated budgets, will return to Mississippi to begin a new phase of work.

"Grass roots people," Moses said, "will enter history." Donna and I will spend the next year just travelling around Mississippi teaching Negroes about themselves, those poor, simple folks on the bottom no one trusts. We'll teach them Negro history. We'll teach them you don't have to know history to make history. We'll

teach them they are more qualified than any professional leader to know how to make a better life for themselves. And I'll get them to write about their lives, and I'll send some of it to you because it will be so poetic."
December 3, 1964

MARCY BENSTOCK: THE WOMAN WHO BLOCKED WESTWAY

The power brokers call her a girl, a fanatic, the Soot Lady, a relic from the sixties. But Marcy Benstock has defied the combined authority of the governor, the mayor, the three daily newspapers, David Rockefeller, the highway lobby, and the real estate industry. She has battled these rapacious dragons to a deadlock, and she will probably slay them in the end.

When Westway, the monster boondoggle, is finally dead and buried, Marcy Benstock will have done more than any other human being to have prevented the squandering of $4 billion of the people's money. And done more to have kept alive the option of an interest-free mass transit trade-in which would salvage the decaying subways.

For eight years, Benstock, now forty, has devoted her whole life to a single issue—beating the highwaymen. The sacrifices have been immense. This Radcliffe graduate with an M.A. in economics has surrendered weekends, vacations, conventional career goals, material comforts, financial security, and much of her personal life. She has lived on $12,000 take-home pay each of the last two years by dressing frugally, eating simply, living in a rent-controlled apartment on West 100th Street, not owning a car and not using taxis, even when traveling alone at night.

Over eight years, Benstock has been evicted from four different offices. She has answered her own phone and raised her own pittance of foundation funding that doesn't even provide for a Xerox machine. She has held press conferences that went unreported. She has conquered her own physical exhaustion and existential dread. But on her pauper's budget, she has out organized and out thought the whole Westway infrastructure, an infrastructure of institutions that has so far spent $64 million on dredging, design, demolition, and hype; disbursed in 1981 more than a million dollars for campaign contributions, public relations, and lobbying; paid at least three million dollars in fees to law firms like Beveridge and Diamond; Shea, Gould; and Cravath, Swaine & Moore; and paid the consulting firm of Lowell Bridwell, the Westway mastermind, $8.8 million in consultant fees.

There have been many, many heroes and heroines in the ten-year resistance to Westway—environmentalists, lawyers, legislators, judges, community activists, journalists, technical experts, government officials. *But only Marcy Benstock has fought Westway, to the exclusion of anything else, for eight years.* In that period, she licked her own envelopes and delivered her own press releases, and kept alive an alternative version of reality and history —until the courts certified it as the truth.

She has educated generations of journalists, converted skeptical administrators into anti-Westway moles, fashioned alliances with businessmen and upstate politicians, and excavated facts out of the bedrock of the bureaucracy, putting them in the hands of key decision makers like Bellamy, Fink, and Ravitch. The debate over Westway has essentially been trench warfare between two competing sets of facts—and Marcy's facts have proven to be the most reliable.

By mastering the arcane technicalities of highway finance and aquatic breeding, she helped crack the cover-up of the highwaymen and their lawyers. Marcy's one-woman organization—the Clean Air Campaign—was an original plaintiff in the federal law suit that led Judge Thomas Griesa to stop all funding for Westway and to nullify all permits for Westway design and construction. She helped convince her friend, Albert Butzel—who has donated most of his time for free—to begin the Westway litigation in 1977, and she has functioned as an investigator/publicist, in day-to-day contact with the lawyers, ever since. Steve Polan, who was Carol Bellamy's Westway conscience and who now works for MTA chairman Richard Ravitch, says: "Marcy is the glue that holds all the Westway opposition together."

Robert Caro, the author of *The Power Broker* and a hero to so many urban writers and reformers, says Marcy is an inspiration to him. "Marcy reminds me of Lillian Edelstein," Caro says, "only Marcy is more sophisticated. And she may do what Lillian couldn't do. She may win." (Lillian Edelstein is the heroine of the "One Mile" chapter in Caro's great book. She was the charismatic East Tremont housewife who led the long, futile grass-roots resistance to Robert Moses's Cross Bronx Expressway during the 1950s.)

Recalls anti-Westway organizer Steve Max: "Marcy has never had any other agenda except Westway. Every week she calls me with a set of tasks. Prepare this testimony. Get that document. Pressure that legislator. Write that letter to the editor. Go to that meeting. Find that fact. She has organized the organizers."

In this age of selfishness, in this city of egos, Marcy Benstock has done all this out of simple altruism and a love of subways. She has gotten nothing from her efforts. She has not run for public office. She has not become a media celebrity, because she is shy and has never pushed herself forward to hog credit. She has not formed a consulting company. She has never received government grants or contracts.

What she has done is to take the lessons she learned twelve years ago in Washington, as a late-blooming apprentice to Ralph Nader—the lessons of citizen action, personal resistance, and material sacrifice—and applied these values here, in New York, to the most expensive planning and public works mistake in memory.

Marcy Benstock grew up in Buffalo, attended private schools, and entered Radcliffe in 1959. She now describes herself as "a dreamy English major. . . . I never read a newspaper in college. I had no idea the Cuban missile crisis was happening. I was interested in how people actually lived, and I only found that out in literature."

So while the civil rights movement of sit-ins and freedom rides was igniting most elite campuses, Marcy resided in the imaginative world of Shakespeare, Arthur Miller, Eugene O'Neill, Chaucer, and George Eliot. The realm of politics only began to open up to Marcy after she graduated and moved to Manhattan's West Side in 1963.

"I became conscious of injustice for the first time by starting to read *The New York Times,*" she recalls. "And I discovered mass transit, the subways, when I moved to New York. I treasured the subways more than the theater or the beaches and parks, or the nice restaurants. I loved looking at the faces each day in the subway cars."

Benstock also began to learn "how people actually lived" by walking around her new neighborhood. "I became very upset by the welfare hotels near my apartment on West 100th Street," she says. But her reaction was not a middle-class backlash. "I was touched by the waste of those people's lives. I had a strong emotional response to human suffering." The name of the welfare hotel closest to her apartment was the Harvard, which probably influenced Marcy more than Harvard University.

The middle 1960s Marcy describes as "a drifting, searching period in my life." She was a consultant to some poverty programs, she did some editing jobs, had periods of unemployment, and over five years she slowly earned an M.A. in economics at the New School. Her teachers included Robert Heilbroner and the late populist senator, Paul Douglas. She also did research for Herb Hill for a book he was writing about blacks and labor. ("I'm sure he doesn't remember me.") She was not attracted to the fight to stop the Lower Manhattan Expressway, or to John Lindsay's reform campaign for mayor in 1965.

People who knew Marcy during this period, as well as those who know her best now, all say the same thing: "There are no Marcy Benstock anecdotes." She seems to have been very private, inner-directed, and self-contained, whether floating through life or giving the permanent government a bloody nose.

In 1969 Marcy applied for—and was given—a job at $75 a week, editing a series of books being written by Ralph Nader's Raiders. She moved to Washington for what she thought would be a three-month assignment, but stayed for twenty-two months, and ended up coauthoring *Water Wasteland* with David Zwick, a study of the government's failure to regulate water pollution.

She also helped edit *Vanishing Air* by John Esposito and Larry Silverman.

"I never got to know Ralph," she says, "but he did become a role model for me. Working for Nader I learned that the laws that are on the books are better than people think they are. The thing to do is to get people to enforce these existing laws through citizen pressure."

Which is a good description of the environmental protection laws and the role Benstock has played in the Westway lawsuit.

Marcy also says of Nader: "He made me feel not crazy to have certain values, because he was acting on those same values in a public way."

Marcy's coauthor, David Zwick, who remains an environmental lawyer, says the thing he remembers most vividly during their twenty-two-month collaboration was her "tenacity."

"The funding for our project ran out four months before we finished the book. So we paid for our own phone calls. Events kept changing and making parts of the book obsolete. So Marcy rewrote sections. The Nixon administration wouldn't give us any information, and put severe restrictions on our interviews. But Marcy hung in there. She really gets angry at the bastards. I think her capacity for righteous anger is what makes her so uncompromising and so relentless."

Benstock says living in Washington was "torture." She missed the parks, old movies, her friends, subways, and the street life of New York. So as soon as the book was completed she moved back to West 100th Street, and in the autumn of 1971 began her life as a public interest organizer. She came to her apartment and found soot all over her books, all over her windowsills. "There was even soot over my contact lenses," she says. But before too long, she started the Upper West Side Air Pollution Campaign, out of a tiny office on West 106th Street. John Lindsay was the mayor, and Jerome Kretchmer was administrator of the Environmental Protection Agency, and their rhetoric was activist government and citizen participation. Marcy tried to hold them to their words. She got the city to promise to conduct an antipollution class in the community if she could get 25 building superintendents to sign up to take it. She got 114. The city started a policy that let citizens initiate complaints against polluters before the

Environmental Control Board. Marcy discovered—and publicized—that the city government had never printed the forms
required to file these complaints. The city printed them, and
Marcy's volunteers filed 500 complaints. She conducted a survey
with volunteers that found 700 oil burners and 300 incinerators
on the West Side were not in compliance with the city's clean
air code. After two years, soot was reduced by 30 percent in a
200-block area.

During this period, Marcy first hooked up with Butzel, now
the lead lawyer on the Westway lawsuit. The city's Environmental Control Board was doing an inadequate job of fining polluters
—a power that it had under the law—so Marcy began a campaign
to get public hearings on nominees to the board and, if possible,
pressure the mayor to appoint some members willing to apply
sanctions against landlords and Con Edison.

"Several people recommended that we try to get Butzel on the
board," Benstock recalls. "So we met with him about 1972. He
had already started his lawsuit over Con Edison's plant at Storm
King, which involved striped bass. He never got nominated, but
I did get to know him, and we've worked together on and off ever
since."

During 1972 and through June 1975, Marcy was funded by
the Fund for the City of New York. Gregory Farrell, the fund's
executive director, met her in 1971, and remains one of her great
admirers.

"I still remember Marcy's first funding proposal to us. She
only wanted to pay herself the legal minimum wage. I had to
convince her that she should propose a slightly higher salary for
herself in her own proposal. I had to persuade her that she could
apply part of her salary to lobbying under the existing tax laws.
In 1973, she only took an annual salary of $7500. The moral
standard she set for herself was very impressive. A lot of people
with good ideas are empire builders. They have grand designs for
expansions, mergers, bigger staffs. Not Marcy. She wanted nothing for herself. In that way she reminds me of Cesar Chavez."

It is an irony that the Fund for the City of New York should
have subsidized, no matter how modestly, Marcy's apprenticeship
as an organizer. Over the years, the fund's board of directors has
been filled with Westway enthusiasts, like Ed Costikyan, Richard

Wade, Alton Marshall, Peter Solomon, Ken Axelson, and current City Corporation Counsel Fritz Schwartz. But Farrell says that no one has ever complained that he nourished this giant killer when she was just the Soot Lady on the West Side.

In May 1975, Michael Gerrard, a transit expert, completed a ninety-four-page evaluation of Marcy Benstock's performance under FCNY funding. After some limited criticism of Marcy's "conspiratorial view of events" and the "personality quirk" of her shyness about fund raising, Gerrard offered this prophetic conclusion:

"I have found a general consensus among those who follow New York environmental politics, which after much study I share: that Marcy Benstock is among the nearly indispensable handful of citizen environmentalists in the city, and her loss would substantially diminish the quality of citizen participation in environmental decision making—and would most likely lead to damage to the environment itself."

Gerrard recommended a new cycle of funding for Benstock's Clean Air Campaign. She did get one last grant in June of 1975, but by the end of that year, Marcy was without a source of funding, just as she was plunging into the effort to stop Westway.

Marcy Benstock vividly remembers the first time she felt emotionally engaged in the Westway issue. It was in the autumn of 1973 when she heard Lowell Bridwell, then director of the West Side Highway project, speak for two hours at a meeting of the West Side community planning board.

"It was his arrogance that struck me," she remembers. "He had a certain kind of slick, self-assured superiority that I found disturbing. He had a scale model of the highway that night, and he made a sophisticated presentation. There was one lawyer at the meeting named David Rothman who tried to ask some questions, and he was shut up. I was upset at the tactics of Bob Kagan, who ran the meeting. And I was furious at Bridwell's contempt for democracy, and his vast skill at intimidating people while appearing to have a reasonable, forthright manner."

Nine years later it would be Bridwell's "contempt for democracy" that would so outrage Judge Griesa when he realized that Bridwell and others had concealed information and "acted in willful derogation of the requirements of law."

Marcy had gone to the 1973 meeting because of her passion for clean air, and the new highway's potential contribution to air pollution through increasing automobile use at the expense of mass transit.

But others had already been sounding the alarm against Westway for almost two years. Arthur Stoliar of the Village planning board was asking the right questions at public meetings as early as January 1972. So was Rachalle Wall, the chairwoman of the Village planning board. Attorney David Rothman began organizing opposition on the West Side, and David Gurin published a seminal anti-Westway essay in the *Village Voice* on November 30, 1972. By the time Marcy's nervous system rebelled at Bridwell's arrogance, the diffuse elements of resistance already existed.

Marcy went to more Westway meetings after that. Mostly she sat in the back and listened. She studied the 1973 enactment into law of the mass transit trade-in provision, which meant interstate highway funds could legally be exchanged for subway and bus subsidies. She did some networking with other early doubters of the boondoggle, like Bunny Gabel, Bill Bowser, and Tom Stokes. When the state's Department of Transportation held four public hearings on Westway in 1974, Marcy attended them all. Whenever a speaker delivered an effective presentation against the highway, Marcy put his or her name on an index card.

By the fall of 1974, Marcy completed her transition from soot to Westway, and helped found ART—Action for Rational Transit, a coalition of fifty-one groups. Working with Bunny Gabel, Steve Max, and Lynn Bender, they united the Greenwich Village and West Side factions opposing Westway, and started to do what Marcy does best—distribute information. At this stage it was information about the brand-new trade-in law for mass transit. She overcame her shyness and began to speak at community board meetings, at public hearings, and even at protest rallies, always without rhetoric, always with facts.

When I asked Marcy what she remembers best about 1975 and 1976, she said it was the struggle to find funding, to make herself permanent and institutional. "I was in a constant panic about survival," Marcy says. "It felt like I spent half my time writing foundation proposals."

Benstock's Clean Air Campaign received its last grant of

$25,000 from the Fund for the City of New York in June 1975. In 1976 she received $10,000 from the Field Foundation; $10,000 from the New York Foundation; and $2500 from the F. W. Beinecke Fund. In 1977, as a result of recommendations from the Joint Foundation Support, she survived on $5000 from the Joyce and John Gutfreund Foundation, and another $5000 from Mrs. Agnes Saalfield. During these same hard times, Marcy lost her office above the Olympia Theater because the rent was raised, and then had to give up a sublease because the building was rehabbed.

In 1977, Ed Koch, who had promised "Westway will never be built," was elected mayor, and Marcy had a moment of optimism. Koch had said it. He had put it in writing. He had made it a campaign promise.

The institutional power and wealth behind Westway has always been awesome. The principal pro-Westway group (New York Citizens for Balanced Transportation) lists among its directors investment banker Felix Rohatyn of Lazard Freres; W. H. James, former publisher of the *Daily News;* Marian Sulzberger Heiskell, sister of *The New York Times* chairman publisher; Richard Shinn, chairman of the Metropolitan Life Insurance Company; William Ellinghaus, president of AT&T: Edward Costikyan, a partner in the Paul, Weiss, Rifkind law firm; David Margolis, president of Colt Industries and Mayor Koch's close friend and leading fund raiser; former mayor Robert Wagner; Gerald Schoenfeld, chairman of the board of the Shubert Organization; and former City Planning Commission chairman Donald Elliot and John Zuccotti.

During the year 1980, this lobbying organization reported to the state attorney general income of $247,000. For the same year, Marcy Benstock's Clean Air Campaign reported income of $29,595. The pro-Westway lobby paid $40,000 just for public relations, and another $40,000 in salary to its executive director. In addition, the Chamber of Commerce, the New York Partnership, the Association for a Better New York, the Regional Plan Association for a Better New York, the Regional Plan Association, all the construction unions, most of the major real estate developers, and the *Times, News,* and *Post* were all part of the lobby.

So, after six months in office, Ed Koch, who has never in his life stuck to a position that might be unpopular or politically disadvantageous, broke his campaign vow and defected to the highwaymen.

I asked Marcy if Koch's betrayal was her psychological low ebb. She said no, there were other periods when she felt even more despairing and pessimistic. "In 1979 I was so depressed I was unable to ask anyone for help," she says. "I was close to giving up. The mayor and the governor were in favor of Westway. I had to give up my sublet at NYPIRG and look for new office space. I was physically very tired. I was feeling responsible for all the different parts of the Westway opposition—legal, administrative, legislative, media, and community. And raising funds to stay alive was still taking up a lot of my time. It was at this low ebb that Pat Hewitt of Joint Foundation Support called me up and asked if I needed some more money. She was the only foundation executive who ever initiated funding."

After more reflection, however, Marcy described a different sort of nadir, a moment of almost existential dread. There came a time when Marcy Benstock, who first acquired her understanding of social wrong in the world partially from reading *The New York Times*, came to dread reading the *Times* on those days she knew there would be a story about Westway.

"I can't get rid of the notion of what *The New York Times* should be," she says. "There was a time in my life when I believed everything that was in the *Times*. Then I started to work on Westway full-time. And I discovered the *Times* published inaccuracies and distortions, and there were omissions that reflected a bias. The *Times* never said *why* the real estate interests wanted Westway. And I know that stories were written and sometimes killed by editors. And that editorials misstated facts about the availability of the mass transit trade-in. The *Times* made Westway seem *inevitable*. About 1978 or 1979 I realized that on those days I knew the *Times* would have a Westway story or editorial, I found myself dreading to read it. I felt so powerless. I just can't protect myself from getting disappointed time after time, by the *Times*. I've accepted everything else about reality except that newspapers lie. I know individual reporters have been fair and taken risks."

The *Times*, in fact, has played a fascinating institutional role in the history of Westway. It published fourteen separate editorials, of increasing certitude, in favor of Westway between 1971 and 1977. Five were published during 1977. On November 14, 1977, the *Times* claimed that "trading in Westway seems to us to offer transit gains that are minimal at best, and questionable in the extreme." And on December 31, 1977, the *Times* said flatly: "We urge Mayor-elect Koch to proceed with Westway," thus encouraging Koch to violate his covenant with the electorate.

John Oakes was the editor of the *Times* editorial page until the end of 1976, and he accepts responsibility for the early editorials on Westway, which at least had a philosophical reserve. But by 1977 Oakes, as a senior editor with more time to think, began to change his mind about Westway. And in 1978 he published three brilliant personal columns against Westway (January 10, February 13, and April 22). It was Marcy Benstock who helped change John Oakes' mind.

"I have material in my files from Marcy going back to 1977," Oakes told me. "I was very impressed with how accurate and complete Marcy's information was. She was very persistent. She kept sending me reports, fact sheets, testimony, documents. No one I know has ever gotten any mistaken information from Marcy. She has referred me to other reliable people, lawyers, and transit experts. I have never met a better supplier of facts in my life than Marcy." Then he added, wistfully, "I wish I had met Marcy while I was still responsible for the *Times'* editorial page."

The *Times'* official editorial policy curiously remains pro-Westway, despite five years of detailed and powerful anti-Westway columns by Tom Wicker (1), Anothey Lewis (3), Sydney Schanberg (7), and Oakes (7). The explanation for this duality seems to be the extraordinary isolation of the *Times'* editorial board. Unlike John Oakes, or Judge Griesa, they have refused to expose their closed minds to Marcy Benstock and her fact factory.

"I've been unable to even get a meeting with the *Times* editorial board," Benstock says. "I wrote a letter to Max Frankel requesting a meeting. And there were follow-up phone calls. But they refused to meet with us."

Another sovereign institution that has been influenced by Benstock has been the New York state legislature, which this year restricted financing for Westway. This restriction was eventually vetoed by Governor Carey. The assembly voted 83 to 55 to override the veto, 17 short of the necessary two-thirds majority.

But 83 votes against Westway had come from a dozen Manhattan reform Democrats.

What began to change the mood and mind of legislature was a fact that Marcy Benstock discovered about two years ago: the federal highway trust fund was running a deficit. This meant not every approved interstate in the country could actually be funded. Thus the 90 percent federal funding for Westway, which Carey, Koch, and the *Times* kept citing as definite, was really doubtful. This meant Westway might be started and never completed— like the Second Avenue subway. This meant the fragile state budget might be invaded to pay for Westway. And if that happened, it would take money away from local projects in Binghamton, Utica, and Watertown. And this suggested to Marcy Benstock there might now be a reason, based on logical self-interest, for upstate legislators to oppose Westway.

How did Marcy discover the federal highway trust fund was in the red?

"I was reading some federal highway administration documents," she said, "and I came across a long memo on the financial status of the highway trust fund. It wasn't confidential. It was just that no one had bothered to read it. Then I got my hands on two more federal highway documents, and one of them said flatly that the completion of the interstate system was an 'unobtainable goal.' Then I got a report from the Congressional Budget Office which provided more information on the trust fund's deficit. For years the supporters of Westway had been saying the trade-in wasn't really available, and suddenly I discovered that it was the money for Westway itself that really wasn't available."

Marcy tried to get this startling fact into the media, but it has never appeared in any daily New York newspaper editorial, although John Oakes did write a column about it in the *Times* last March. In 1981 she began her campaign to convince the legislature that the state would have to divert funds from upstate roads and highways in order to build Westway in Manhattan.

Benstock made her first visit to Albany in March 1981, bringing the official list of all planned interstate projects in the state and their funding estimates to prove her diversion-for-Westway argument. She had gotten the list by walking into the state's Department of Transportation office at 2 World Trade Center and asking for the "cost estimate books." She duplicated the pages, retyped them herself on a single page, and took the piece of paper with her up to Albany. She went to Albany with a delegation that included Seymour Durst, the landlord who has been so active in the Westway opposition, and Walter Beebee, a lawyer. They lobbied Republican legislators, including Senator James Donovan, the ultraconservative foe of abortion. A year later Donovan would put out a press release opposing Westway.

Marcy also met with Assembly Speaker Stanley Fink, who was then just beginning his slow, wavering turn against Westway. There are no more opposite personalities than the tough, gruff, wise-cracking, impatient, pragmatic Fink, and the scholarly, sedate, idealistic, obsessive, relentless Benstock. But Fink's staff says Marcy's avalanche of facts did make an impact, although Marcy remembers that Fink, who sometimes likes to mask his liberalism, called her a "do-gooder."

In June 1981 Benstock sent a Westway memo to every member of the legislature, which she now admits was "incomprehensible. . . . I tried to document information nobody understands. I'm sure most of them never even read it. It was eight single-spaced pages, so it wouldn't seem so long."

And through 1981 Marcy had more and more contacts with Fink's excellent staff, especially Bob Kurtter and David Langdon. The fact factory was working overtime, and staff was translating the product into consensus politics for their boss.

In March 1982, Marcy went back to Albany for three intensive days of lobbying. *New York Post* reporter Barbara Ross recalls Marcy's visit: "Marcy was originally going to stay at the Howard Johnson motel. But she switched to a cheaper motel in town to save money and to avoid the $4 taxi fare to the Capitol. She had one skirt and one sweater for three days. She had almost no money, so I took her to lunch. In a way, she must have looked like a waif."

While Marcy was in Albany there was a Westway debate in the closed Democratic caucus between William Hennessey, the state transportation commissioner, and Richard Gottfried, the West Side assemblyman. Marcy briefed Gottfried. She helped him prepare a visual chart that illustrated New York's percentage share of the shrinking national pot of highway money. She gave him copies of the documents that analyze the deficit in the highway trust fund. By all accounts Gottfried was magnificent and routed Hennessey.

The next day there was a climactic meeting in Fink's hideaway office between the Speaker and the hard core of anti-Westway Democrats. This was the meeting that would decide if Fink would go along with the budget restrictions on Westway financing.

"A couple of assemblymen tried to smuggle me into the meeting," Marcy recalls. "But Fink kicked me out. So I sat in a small reception area and listened to the heated voices and loud arguing coming from behind the locked door. I sat there for more than an hour arranging my stack of documents, trying to anticipate which fact I would need to rebut Fink. Suddenly the legislators rushed out of the room, and I knew it was going to be okay, because Gottfried, Denny Farrell, and the others were all smiling."

On October 19, 1973—almost nine years ago—Marcy Benstock wrote a memo to Gregory Farrell, at the Fund for the City of New York. She wrote that "environmental lawsuits have caused costly delays in highway construction," and then offered the cooperation of her Clean Air Campaign to the city to avert such a lawsuit over Westway. Late in 1974, Action for Rational Transit (ART), the coalition of fifty-one groups organized by Marcy, filed a lawsuit to stop Westway on the grounds that it violated the Clean Air Act of 1970. But the Clean Air Campaign itself was not a plaintiff in that litigation, and Albert Butzel was not the attorney, because he and Marcy wanted to be free to sue at a later date. Marcy and Butzel did not launch their lawsuit against Westway until June 27, 1979.

At 11:45 A.M. on Wednesday, June 30, 1982, Benstock reluctantly left her phone unattended in her two-room office at 150 Nassau Street that she shares with the *Credit Union News*. She began her ten-minute walk to the federal courthouse at Foley Square to obtain a copy of Judge Thomas Griesa's latest opinion in the Westway case. She was tense. She was not sure how favorable it would be. She had sat through a two-week trial and observed Griesa grow more and more enraged at what he called the fraud and deception of the pro-Westway witnesses. But Griesa is a hard judge to anticipate. He is an intellectually conservative man, a Nixon appointee from a Wall Street firm, a believer in the system. He also is a strict moralist who can't abide lying, or those who cheat on the law.

All during the trial, Marcy had tried to get the press to pay attention. She called reporters from the three daily papers and two wire services. The *Times* even sent two reporters to attend the trial. But no story was ever published. So for two weeks Marcy watched the Westway cover-up unraveling before her eyes, with witnesses under oath and a court reporter making a transcript. But it was not getting into the papers. It was vindication in a vacuum.

One afternoon I had watched Marcy's arch nemesis—suave, contemptuous Lowell Bridwell—on the stand and I heard him admit that he had intentionally withheld information from the U.S. Army Corps of Engineers because Westway critics would then be legally entitled to it under the Freedom of Information Act.

At exactly noon on June 30, Judge Griesa's clerk gave Marcy a copy of the fifty-two-page opinion that Carol Bellamy would call "the final nail in Westway's coffin."

The decision was more comprehensive and more lucid than Marcy ever dared hope. It said that all previous federal approval of Westway funds, design, and location was "null and void." And it said that the testimony of Bridwell and two other defense witnesses "was characterized not only by a striking lack of plausibility on critical points, but also by a remarkable amount of inconsistency, evasion, and asserted loss of memory on matters where memory would be expected." Judge Griesa's decision said the state's environmental impact statement was false, and that it should have been corrected but wasn't.

Marcy Benstock did not go to the nearest bar and have a celebratory drink. She walked briskly back to her cluttered office and started purposefully to call the press, to notify them of the decision, and of a 2:30 P.M. press conference with Butzel, Mitch Bernard, the other attorney on the case, and most of the original plaintiffs.

Marcy keeps a little file box on her desk, with index cards for more than a hundred people in the media, with small notations on some of the cards about past stories the person has written about Westway.

Calmly, methodically, Marcy started calling the names on

these index cards, starting with the dailies who had neglected her pleas to report on the trial, and then to the wire services, then the *Washington Post,* the *Wall Street Journal.*

Her friend Bunny Gabel of Friends of the Earth agreed to help make some of the calls from her home. Then radio news departments started calling and asking Marcy for telephone beeper interviews. She had to politely decline, and continue her disciplined phoning: John Hess, Joe Conason, the *Westsider,* the *Staten Island Advance,* every reporter who has ever mentioned Westway seemed to be in Marcy's file box.

Finally it was 2:15 and Marcy was late for her victory press conference. She headed straight for the IRT and rode uptown on her beloved and decaying subway.

August 3, 1982

MUHAMMAD ALI

Float like a butterfly. Sting like a bee. And exit like a hero.

Muhammad Ali, after many rehearsals, is reportedly ready to retire for good, nineteen years after winning an Olympic gold medal for America as Cassius Clay.

We have burdened Ali with many identities. Symbol of the sixties. Draft dodger. Muslim evangelist. Most famous human on earth. Exile. People's champ. Braggart. Huckster. Manchild. Poet. Rebel. Survivor. He can be as funny as Richard Pryor. He can be as eloquent as Jesse Jackson. He is as charismatic as the Ayatollah.

But basically he is a fighter, the greatest fighter of the age. He danced like Nureyev. He could stick like Manolete. And he could think like Einstein.

What follows are basically a fan's notes, a farewell tribute to a public man who gave me pleasure, who gave me memories that are treasured. A man who showed how a life might be lived, and what personal values are important.

Twelve years ago this week—on April 28, 1967—Ali refused to take the "one step forward" at his army induction center in Houston, Texas. At that moment in history, the Vietnam war was still a popular war. And the Black Muslims to which Ali belonged were perceived by white America as a menacing and alien conspiracy. That same day, the New York State Athletic Commission withdrew its official recognition of Ali as heavyweight champion of the planet and suspended his license. Ali was not yet arraigned, indicted, tried, or convicted. He was never given a hearing or time for an appeal. He was stripped of his crown by a press release.

For three and a half years he was not allowed to fight. Ali and his lawyers drifted around the country like vagabonds looking for a location that would let him work. Seventy-two cities refused to give him a license. Seattle and Detroit were close to letting him fight, but then the politicians and vigilantes held press conferences, and the permission evaporated. No white politician in the land would go on record to defend Ali's right to fight. He went broke. And he was robbed of his prime. We will never see what Ali was like between the ages of twenty-five and twenty-eight, because he was not permitted to work during the three years that an athlete's body is at its peak.

Three memories.

The first time I saw Ali was in the March of 1963, at Madison Square Garden. He had already knocked out Archie Moore and was promised a chance at the champ, Sonny Liston, if he could beat Doug Jones that night in the old Fiftieth Street Garden. I had worked at the Garden a few years before and was able to acquire a free ticket to see the twenty-one-year-old kid still named Cassius Clay.

Jones was a solid professional. He had recently knocked out Bob Foster, and the contest with Jones was a hard, close fight. But one could glimpse Ali's unripe genius that night. He had the fastest hands I ever saw. He seemed to have a built-in radar system that helped him slip punches at the last second. He charmed the crowd with the antic Ali Shuffle. And he could dance all night. He was on his toes all ten rounds. That night, on display as a work-in-progress, was Ali's original and distinctive style.

The Ali style of Constant Movement—dancing, sticking the jab, throwing a fast, hurtful combination, dancing to the left, dancing to the right, sticking, moving—this method would revolutionize boxing the way that Charlie Parker's bop improvisations changed jazz, or Hemingway's spare cadences influenced a generation of writers. Watch Sugar Ray Leonard, the fighter of the future, and you will see the echo of Muhammad.

After he won the close decision, in his dressing room, Ali recited his latest poem: "Don't bet on Sonny, and save your money." A year later, Ali, an 8-to-1 underdog, knocked out Sonny Liston.

In the autumn of 1967, I saw Ali speak at a college in Chicago. A smart-ass questioner asked him: "Isn't it a contradiction for you to participate in a violent sport like boxing but object to the violence in Vietnam? What's the difference?"

Ali's reply, which seemed spontaneous to me, was: "Man, there ain't no referees in Vietnam, that's the difference."

In September of 1970, I wrote a *Voice* piece on Ali. I spent two days with him and was struck by his sense of himself as a historical figure, and by his understanding of how much he is a symbol and vessel of the dreams of blacks all over the world. He had just seen Howard Sackler's play about Jack Johnson, *The Great White Hope,* and he kept saying that he would "never go out as a loser" the way Jack Johnson did, the way Joe Louis did, the way Sugar Ray Robinson did. Ali has a powerful sense of racial history and symbolism, and he has a perfect sense of this history as it applies to boxing. He has said that only white heavyweight champions Gene Tunney and Rocky Marciano retired with the title. He wants to be the first great black champion to do this. And that is why, despite the $10 million temptation of one last big fight, it appears that he soon will retire—with the crown in his custody.

Ali's secret asset has been his pride, his will to win, and his self-knowledge. God gave him the hand speed and the gift of dancing legs. But time inevitably eroded Ali's body; it was diminished during his three and a half years of exile; and then he had to use up everything he held in reserve to win the third epic war with Joe Frazier. But as age deteriorated Ali's natural gifts, he began to create new ways to win.

Ali is like Picasso. He has gone through three or four different periods, adding different philosophies and colors to his palette through the years. He beat Doug Jones with his youth. He beat Cleveland Williams with his punching power. He beat Joe Frazier with his heart. He beat George Foreman with his imagination. He beat Leon Spinks with his memory.

But to me, the most impressive quality that Ali has is the way he has survived defeat, handled defeat emotionally, and come back from it stronger than ever.

Losing is the hardest thing of all for an athlete. Losing a fight, which is one on one, where you can't blame a teammate, is the most crushing form of defeat to accept and come to terms with. One defeat destroyed George Foreman's whole career. He believed he was invincible. When he lost for the first time, his self-confidence could not be restored and he disintegrated as a boxer.

Three fighters over nineteen years managed to defeat Ali: Ken Norton, Joe Frazier, and Leon Spinks. And Ali beat each of them in return bouts. Ali's pride was able to recover from defeat, learn from it; he was driven to redeem himself from each loss. Ali believed in his own myth even more than his fans did. The myth said he was "The Greatest."

Ali loved fun too much to endure the pain and boring discipline of training. The three times he lost he did not train faithfully. But for each rematch with a conqueror, he punished his body in training. At six in the morning, no one knows whether you have run two miles or six miles. Ali ran the six miles. Out of pride. He went to the woodshed three times and rebuilt his ego.

In his book *The Greatest*, Ali described his hospitalization after Ken Norton broke his jaw. In the hospital, he received a gloating note that said: "THE BUTTERFLY HAS LOST ITS WINGS, THE BEE HAS LOST ITS STING. You are through, you loudmouthed braggart. Your mouth has been shut for all times. It's a great day for America. You are finished."

Ali wrote: "Later I tape it up on the wall of the gym so that every day I train, I remember the butterfly has got to get back its wings and the bee has to get back its sting. Of all the messages that came into me while I was in Claremont Hospital, this is the one I like best. It's funny, but those who hate me the most sometimes inspire me the most."

When Ali's reflexes began to slow, when his magical radar screen broke down, he learned and perfected other skills. Like taking a punch. In 1974, he treated his hands sore with calcium deposits, with hot wax and cortisone. This added to his punching power as his legs lost their spring.

When he confronted Foreman in Zaïre, Ali was the betting underdog. He psyched the unstable Foreman by leading the black African multitude between rounds in the "Ali! Ali! Bomaye!" chant. He made the crowd his choir. He invented the rope-a-dope strategy in the second round and let Foreman punch himself into panting exhaustion. This tactic was an improvisation of Ali's and he stuck with it despite handlers' pleadings that he abandon it.

The Ali who met Spinks last September was a chess player. His speed was almost all gone. He was nearly thirty-seven years old. Spinks, at twenty-five, had beaten him seven months earlier. But Ali possessed self-knowledge. He knew his body. He knew exactly how much stamina he had left, how many seconds of each round he could dance, how many punches he had to throw to win each round. He was a genius-miser with his hoarded energy; he spent just enough to win a round, just enough to deflate Spinks' confidence, just enough to dominate the fight mentally.

When he beat Spinks, Ali won the heavyweight championship of the world for the third time. Nobody in the history of sports had ever accomplished that.

Brecht said we should pity the land that needs heroes. But I think heroes are valuable, and necessary. Ali is a saving remnant of heroism.

He was the best in the world at what he did. He has class. He has principles he suffered for. He proved that courage, self-knowledge, and determination can prevail against great odds. He said no to the Vietnam war at a time when wise men from Harvard were bombing women and children. He gave, through his exploits, a feeling of dignity to the dispossessed and the hopeless.

Float like a butterfly. Sting like a bee. And go out a winner.
April 30, 1979

DEBTS TO DECLARE, TEACHERS TO THANK

The dream of numerous politicians and felons came true on April 13 at the Village Gate: Jack Newfield, Voice senior editor, was roasted as "the conscience of New York." Unfortunately, most of the roasters, well aware that Newfield has many good years ahead of him, chose to go easy. Following are Jack's remarks to the assembled crowd of 450.

I would like to take this occasion to declare, in a public way, a few debts I feel I owe and to celebrate five mentors and heroes of mine. These teachers have given me a feeling of continuity and tradition, which has been nourishing to me.

The *Village Voice* has provided me with the three most uncommon and precious luxuries a journalist can have—time, space, and freedom. I am forever grateful to almost all the editors of the *Voice* I have worked under: to David Schneiderman, to Marianne Partridge, to Tom Morgan, and to Dan Wolf. The only exception—and in honesty I must say it—was Clay Felker, who suppressed the editorial I wrote endorsing Bella Abzug in the 1976 Senate primary. Jimmy Breslin recently interred Felker, labeling him "the Michael Cimino of journalism."

David, Marianne, and Tom all brilliantly protected the fragile freedom, diversity, and editorial independence of our paper. I was once asked to explain the secret of preserving the *Voice's* independence. I replied that our secret was that we chose to act as if all publishers came from office temporaries.

The reason I have never been sued successfully is Victor Kovner. He is simply the best libel counsel on earth. If Victor didn't exist, the *Village Voice* would probably today be owned by an offshore trust composed of the ten worst judges, John Murphy, and the heirs of Anastasio Somoza. Some day I will test Victor's genius and compose an article called "the ten worst doctors."

When I was growing up in Bed-Stuy, it was reading Jimmy Cannon that made me want to be a journalist. But it was reading

I. F. Stone that made me want to become an intellectual, that made me want to know and study history, that made me respect educated writing.

Over the years, I have learned to read every document carefully because of the example of Izzy Stone. Izzy taught me that detail is everything; that facts, by themselves, can be liberating. Getting detail from documents is the only way to prevent politicians from using you as a stenographer for their deceits. To me, Izzy represents the ideal synthesis of Thomas Jefferson, John Milton, Rosa Luxembourg, and Sherlock Holmes.

Izzy's personal code of conduct during the haunted fifties should serve as an inspiration to all of us during this cold new decade. Izzy never compromised his beliefs to gain legitimacy, access, or cultural patronage. Izzy never named names. And Izzy never joined with those authoritarians who would crush freedom of thought, freedom of the press, or the freedom to form an independent trade union in the name of socialism.

Izzy has had the independence to tell his readers things they did not want to hear. He has had the courage to maintain complex positions, and thereby risk being misunderstood by those seeking the comfort of simplicity and illusion.

Izzy Stone has been much more than the conscience of a city. To me, he has been the conscience of the left.

At every criminal trial, at every public hearing, I look to see if Murray Kempton is there. Then I listen in the hope I might learn or borrow something, from the man I call the Charlie Parker of conversation.

Murray's columns have shown me a very important connection—how to take the crucial political insight that social change comes from below, not above, and translate it into reporting.

In 1956, Murray went to Montgomery to interview Rosa Parks. He did not go to Washington to get a background briefing from J. Edgar Hoover. Reading Murray, I discovered that outsiders really are closer to reality than insiders; that victims know things executioners don't. And so, when I wanted to understand the nursing home rackets, I talked to the nurses' aides who bandaged the infected bedsores of Bergman's patients. When I wanted to identify the bigoted, malingering, and unfit judges, I went to cops and Legal Aid attorneys. When I wanted to understand how Jay Goldin and Jack Bronston rigged the bus shelter bid, I talked to a civil service auditor. And when I wanted to understand the plague of lead poisoning, I went to the South Bronx and interviewed a woman whose twenty-two-month-old daughter had just died of lead poisoning because of a landlord's callous neglect.

Murray Kempton has also instructed me by his inexhaustible, daily routine—that you do your absolute best on every assignment, out of pride and honor, no matter who owns the company. I will not forget what Murray said a few years ago, when he was given the A. J. Liebling prize. It is the credo of a craftsman.

"You are never secure from the accidental attention of somebody who might know. The only final importance of newspapers may very well be that people leave them on subways; and, on the lonely, morose grumble of the Rockaway line, some Richard Wright, some James T. Farrell, some Hart Crane, some Norman Mailer, some Grace Paley—in the guise of an adolescent, with his time to come—may pick you up—and by heaven, you have a duty to be ready for cross-examination."

In my memory, I carry three images of perfection. One is Jackie Robinson stealing home with the bases loaded in Ebbets Field. Another is Sugar Ray Robinson giving away ten pounds and knocking out Jake LaMotta to win the middleweight championship. And the third is the column Murray Kempton wrote the day after Don Larsen pitched his perfect game in the 1956 World Series. Murray's column was not about Larsen. It was about forty-year-old Sal Maglie, who had pitched a glorious two-hitter in that game, and still lost.

Dan Wolf was the shy, passive editor who took a chance and hired me for the *Voice* in the autumn of 1964, after I had flunked my summer tryout on the *New York Post;* and after I had been fired as editor of the *West Side News;* and after I had been fired as a copy boy for the *Daily Mirror.*

Dan's unique approach was that he edited consciousness instead of editing copy. He taught me to question all conventional wisdom, all sacred cows, and all double standards. He cured me of innocence and prepared me to recognize the unexpected when I saw it. He printed ideas and opinions he disapproved of. And he made the *Voice* a writers' newspaper—which meant a young writer felt free to make mistakes and was not restricted by self-censorship.

I regret that I haven't seen Dan much the last few years. But he now works for the fellow who thinks the Constitution is dumb.

But I still prize those gifts of skepticism and intellectual curiosity that Dan gave me during my apprenticeship. I think it was probably inevitable that I would now be using Dan's valued gifts to hold this mayor accountable for his double standards toward blacks and whites.

I can still recall the first time I heard Mike Harrington speak. I was a mesmerized sophomore at Hunter College. In June of 1961, I was arrested with Mike and about fifteen other people in a civil rights sit-in. We all spent the night together in the 20th precinct, listening to Mike lecture about the other Americans. Later that year, I assisted Mike in editing a small, democratic-socialist newspaper called *New America*. For me, that experience was the moral equivalent of graduate school.

Mike Harrington is the person who proves that good politics and good character can coexist in one individual. The clarity of Mike's logic and the integrity of his scholarship are as awesome today as they seemed twenty years ago, in a holding cell on West Fifty-fourth Street.

It's been written in several books that I was some sort of radicalizing influence on Robert Kennedy. The truth, of course, is that he was a much greater influence on me than I ever was on him. And I suspect that is true of everyone who was ever described as "an adviser to Robert Kennedy." He was so much smarter, and tougher, and more capable of growth than the rest of us.

Robert Kennedy expanded my thinking about many things. He gave me my first education into the political economy of organized crime. He told me about Sidney Korshak's shadow world, where businessmen act like gangsters, and gangsters act like businessmen. He opened my eyes to how the Teamsters union often cheated its members and collaborated with employers, years before I wrote about John Cody and Local 282. I first got to know Cesar Chavez and his heroic union through Robert Kennedy. And I heard Kennedy speak in favor of decentralization and local control before Ronald Reagan became the governor of California.

I think the saddest sight I have ever seen was the view from Robert Kennedy's funeral train as it traveled through New Jersey. I saw tens of thousands of poor blacks weeping on one side of the railroad tracks, and tens of thousands of almost poor whites saluting and waving American flags on the other side of the train.

To this day, I keep searching for another leader who might reconcile and reunite those two injured classes, now trapped on separate sides of imaginary tracks.

April 22, 1981

MY JOURNALISTIC ANCESTORS

After participating in several panel discussions, attending *(More's)* counterconvention, reading books and articles by Tom Wolfe and Mike Arlen, and being interviewed by several high school students about it, I have finally come to the conclusion that the New Journalism does not exist. It is a false category. There is only good writing and bad writing, smart ideas and dumb ideas, hard work and laziness.

Anyone who is less than thirty-five and owns a typewriter becomes known as a New Journalist. Writers as different as Richard Goldstein, Eldridge Cleaver, and Rex Reed get lumped together under a contrived umbrella.

Everyone has a different definition of what the New Journalism is. It's the use of fictional techniques, it's composite characterization, it's the art form that's replacing the novel, which is dying. Or it's anyone who used to write for the old *Herald Tribune* magazine, it's participation in the event by the writer, it's the transcendence of objectivity, it's anyone who hangs out at the Lion's Head.

Seymour Krim, in a piece in *New American Review,* once made a reference to the "Cleaver-Rubin-Newfield style." And Mike Arlen linked me and Tom Wolfe together: "The New Journalist is in the end, I think, less a journalist than an impresario. Tom Wolfe presents Phil Spector! Jack Newfield presents Nelson Rockefeller! Norman Mailer presents the Moon Shot!"

This piece is to explain why I don't think there is such a thing as New Journalism, and why I don't think I'm a New Journalist.

To begin with, there is not that much new about the New Journalism. Advocacy preceded the who-what-when-where-why of the AP by a couple of centuries. Tom Paine and Voltaire were New Journalists. So was John Milton when he wrote his "Areopagitica" against government censorship in the seventeenth century. "Objective" journalism developed with the teletype and radio news.

Defoe, Addison and Steele, Stephen Crane, and Mark Twain were all New Journalists according to most definitions. So was Karl Marx when he wrote for the *Herald Tribune.*

Yet something different and better does seem to have happened to mass publication journalism in the last fifteen years. I suspect it is nothing more profound than a lot of good writers coming along at the same time, and a few wise editors like Dan Wolf, Clay Felker, and William Shawn giving these writers a lot of space and freedom to express a point of view. I wouldn't refine the generality much more than that.

But this new rush of talent did not, as Tom Wolfe seems to suggest, spring Zeus-like from John Hay Whitney's banker's brow in the *Trib's* protean city room in the late 1950s, and to have been motivated by an economic desperation to compete with *Playboy's* sexist centerfolds, then attracting considerable advertising revenue away from *Esquire.*

It was during this period that *Esquire* published brilliant profiles of Joe DiMaggio, Frank Sinatra, and Joe Louis by Gay Talese. Talese managed to get inside his subjects' private and interior lives, and give readers a deeper, truer sense of how things really are. At the same time Tom Morgan, now Mayor Lindsay's press secretary, wrote equally rich portraits of Roy Cohn, David Susskind, and Sammy Davis, Jr. These are preserved in a forgot-

ten book, *Self Creations: 13 Impersonalities,* which some paper-
back publisher should wake up and reissue.

Then in 1960 an *Esquire* editor named Clay Felker had an
idea, and assigned Norman Mailer to cover a real event, the
Democratic national convention in Los Angeles. Mailer's piece
was a masterwork of good writing and clear thinking. It was not
a new form. John Hersey, also a novelist, had written about a real
event—Hiroshima. George Orwell had written about the Spanish
civil war. James Agee had written about the life of white tenant
farmers in *Let Us Now Praise Famous Men.*

So Mailer, who happened to be a novelist of distinction, wrote
a great work of journalism. And *Esquire,* in an economic war with
Playboy, published all 30,000 words. I was attending Hunter
College then, and Mailer's piece blew my mind. It also blew Pete
Hamill's and Jimmy Breslin's. Mailer opened a door with that
piece, and the one he did on the Liston-Patterson fight. But it was
not a new art form. He did not invent anything. He just wrote
great liberating prose. Just like Lillian Ross, or Joe Mitchell, or
A. J. Liebling, or Westbrook Pegler, or H. L. Mencken.

I grew up on three journalists: Murray Kempton, sportswriter
Jimmy Cannon, and I. F. Stone. From Kempton I tried to learn
irony and a sense of history; from Cannon a love for the city and
a sense of drama; from Stone a reverence for facts, truth, and
justice. Later, from Hamill and Breslin, I would learn the legitimacy of rage, the folly of politeness, and a sense of concreteness
about the lives of ordinary people.

Then along comes Tom Wolfe, the Boswell of the boutiques,
with a history of the New Journalism that never mentions Kempton, Cannon, or Stone. Or Lillian Ross and Joe Mitchell, who
wrote for the rival *New Yorker.* Or any *Voice* writer, for that
matter. Like any faithful Boswell, Wolfe only mentions his
friends.

I've had a lot of shop talk conversations with Hamill and
Breslin, and both feel a special debt to Cannon for the shaping
of their craft. Hamill, in fact, dedicated his collection, *Irrational
Ravings,* to Cannon.

This is how Pete described Cannon's influence on him: "But
it was Cannon who made me want to be a newspaperman. He
wrote a sports column, but it was always more than that. In some

ways the hero of the column was its style, an undisciplined personal mixture of New York street talk, soaring elegance, Hemingway and Algren, deep Celtic feeling, city loneliness, Prohibition violence, and a personal belief in honor."

But is the seventy-year-old Jimmy Cannon a New Journalist? Or just a good one?

Another, exceptional sportswriter of the fifties left his mark on many of us: W. C. Heinz. Heinz's classic 1952 piece on Rocky Graziano can be found in the anthology *The Best of Sport*, published by Viking. Heinz also authored a lean, beautiful novel about boxing, *The Professional*. Breslin calls Heinz "the best I ever saw." Yet Wolfe and most students of the New Journalism have never even heard of him.

What's called the New Journalism is really a dozen different styles of writing. Talese and Capote do one thing very well. Rex Reed has his own act. Breslin, Hamill, and I have certain things in common—a populist politics, working-class backgrounds, respect for Mailer, Kempton, Cannon, and Heinz, and a love for this wounded city. Sometimes I think the three of us, one pusher, and one junkie will be the last five people left in this town.

And Tom Wolfe represents another strand in all this. He is a gifted, original writer, but he has the social conscience of an ant. Wolfe is a dandy. His basic interest is the flow of fashion, in the tics and trinkets of the rich.

But if Wolfe represents a conservative, or perhaps apolitical approach, there is also the committed school of Stone, Kempton, Royko, Halberstam, Wicker, Cowar, Hentoff and many others.

Some alleged New Journalists, like Robin Reisig and James Ridgeway, are really part of an older muckraking tradition that stretches back to Lincoln Steffens and Ida Tarbell. So is Jack Anderson, who is considered an "old journalist" because he has a syndicated daily column.

Actually, I think the only really new journalism in America today is being done by people like Studs Terkel and Robert Coles, who are trying to record history from the bottom, through the eyes of average, unfamous people, rather than through presidents and celebrities.

Paul Cowan's recent stories on coal miners and the residents of Forest Hills are also in this democratic vein. So are my own prison articles, where I try to present the prison reality from the point of view of powerless unknown inmates, rather than wardens, or expert penologists, or corrections bureaucrats, or liberal politicians.

The New Journalism is not going to become an evolutionary substitute for the novel, as Norman Podhoretz first suggested in a 1958 essay, "The Article as Art." Tom Wolfe also made this excessive claim in his recent essay in *New York* magazine.

The New Journalism, Wolfe wrote, "is causing panic, dethroning the novel as the number one literary genre, starting the first new direction in American literature in half a century."

Nonsense.

First of all, there are still plenty of fine novelists around—Barth, Roth, Updike, Bellow, Ellison, Pynchon, and Malamud are all working. Plus fresh talents on the way up like Fred Exley, Robert Stone, Marge Piercy, Sol Yurick, and Robert Coover, who assure the vitality of the genre.

Second, some of the best New Jouranlists have found their own expanded form still so inhibiting they have turned to writing novels themselves—Hamill, Breslin, Joan Didion, Jeremy Larner, David Halberstam, Joe McGinnis, and earlier, Mailer, Baldwin, and Heinz; Breslin and Joe Flaherty have spent the last year working on novels.

Third, most of us alleged New Journalists have read a lot of naturalistic novels, and have been influenced by Dreiser, Dos Passos, Farrell, Steinbeck, and Algren. This tradition seems out of fashion now, but what's called the New Journalism owes a lot of dues to it.

There is room for both good novels and good journalism. The need for newness, the competition of categories, is just a game of egos. Why deny our roots? What is the need to claim historical novelty? What's wrong with giving credit to Jimmy Cannon and John Steinbeck?

The distinction has also been blurred between what is called New Journalism and underground journalism. If New Journalism can at least be recognized as good writing and lucid thinking, there is little of that in most of the underground press. (I exempt sea-level papers like Boston's *Phoenix* and Chicago's *Daily Planet*.)

EVO proved that postlinear heads couldn't write linear prose.

The dumbest political column of the year—even worse than Evans and Novak—was Al Goldstein's romanticization of George Wallace in the *New York Ace* two issues back.

Most political writers for most underground papers don't know how things really work, and lack the Breslin-Hamill instinct for the concrete. At this point, conventional "old journalism"— like David Broder, Jim Perry, Alan Otten, Martin Nolan, and Mary McGrory write better and see clearer than the underground pundits.

The underground press has been very good at writing about certain things—the war, women's liberation, prisons, rock music. But it has been very bad reporting on other things—electoral politics, original muckraking, neighborhoods and ordinary people, crime and the fear of crime, and excesses and arrogance when they appear on the left.

It was *Life* magazine that broke the Abe Fortas and San Diego scandals. It was Hamill's piece in *New York* magazine (April 14, 1969) that first noticed the swelling rage in white workingmen's neighborhoods. It was the *Staten Island Advance* that first exposed the horror of Willowbrook. It was Jack Anderson who exposed ITT. These are the sort of stories a better underground press might have dug out first.

Some press critics have tried to make "advocacy" the line that divides "biased, irresponsible" New Journalism from professional, objective mainstream journalism. But it seems to me that the most blatant, advocacy journalists have almost always been on the right.

Joe Alsop has been advocating (and predicting) an American military victory in Vietnam for a decade. William F. Buckley might be the purest advocacy journalist in the country. He helped elect his brother to the Senate in 1970. He campaigned for John Ashbrook in New Hampshire this year. He is editor of a magazine with an ideological line much more narrow and rigid than the *Voice.* He even ran for mayor in 1965.

Somehow the concept of advocacy in journalism has become identified with the left. But what about the *Reader's Digest?* They've published seventy-seven pieces on Vietnam since 1951, seventy-six of them in favor of the war. Does *U.S. News and World Report* present a balanced view of capitalism? Is New Hampshire's *Manchester Union Leader* fair and objective?

Objectivity can be defined as the way the mass media reported the history of the Vietnam war before the Pentagon Papers; the way the racism in the North was covered before Watts; the way auto safety was reported before Ralph Nader. Objectivity is the media printing Nelson Rockefeller's lies about Attica until the facts came out that the state troopers and not the inmates had killed all the hostages; that the troopers used outlawed dum dum bullets; that 350 inmates, including some badly wounded, were beaten after they gave up. Objectivity is printing a dozen stories about minor welfare frauds, but not a word about the My Lai massacre until Seymour Hersh. Objectivity is not covering the stomping of gay activists at the Inner Circle dinner because Micky Maye's union paid for a table. Objectivity is ignoring George McGovern as a joke after he won the Wisconsin primary. Objectivity is believing people with power and printing their press releases. Objectivity is not shouting "liar" in a crowded country.

And in the current (May) issue of *(More)*, Robin Reisig has a powerful piece on all the daily "objective" reporters in New York who are on the take.

Harry Schlegel is an assistant city editor on the *Daily News*. He also holds a $900 a month job as research director of the state legislature's joint Committee on Interstate Cooperation. The chairman of the committee is John Marchi, whom the *News* endorsed for mayor in 1969.

George Douris is the City Hall bureau chief for the *Long Island Press*. He also gets paid by the PBA to edit their paper *Front and Center*. And he writes a lot of stories for the *Press* about the police department's fight for higher pay and other matters. They are usually propolice. That's what I would call real personal, participatory journalism.

When Ms. Reisig confronted Douris with his conflict of interest, Douris, with unconscious irony, threatened to call a cop if she didn't leave the City Hall press room.

At bottom, I believe objectivity is a fig leaf for covert prejudice. The point is not to confuse objectivity with truth. It was objective to quote Joe McCarthy during the 1950s; it was the truth to report that most of what he had to say was unfounded slander. Today much of what Nixon, Humphrey, and Rockefeller say is lies, but they are quoted without challenge, and given credibility.

The goal for all journalists should be to come as close to the truth as possible. But the truth does not always reside exactly in the middle. Truth is not the square root of two balanced quotes. I don't believe I should be "objective" about racism, or the conditions inside Clinton Prison, or lead poisoning, or the fact that parts of Brownsville look like Quang Tri. Certain facts are not morally neutral.

A few cynics argue that the New Journalism can best be detected by its resemblance to fiction, by its liberties with the facts. Well, if that's the case, then the best example of New Journalism this season is Edward O'Neill's story in—of all places —the *Daily News,* four Sundays ago.

O'Neill's story was about the Inner Circle dinner. It ran in the first edition that rolls off the presses at 7 P.M. It was a fine story with nice details. The only problem is that the Inner Circle dinner started at 9 P.M. So the story must have been written at least three hours before the dinner actually took place. O'Neill wrote:

"The annual show played to a glittering, laughing-room-only audience of top city and state officials headed by Governor Rockefeller and Mayor Lindsay. Both chuckled heartily as the newsmen satirized Rocky's current "Love Story" with President Nixon."

Rockefeller never showed up, and the *News* story, of course, didn't mention the beating of the gay activists at the dinner. But O'Neill should soon start receiving invitations to lecture on the New Journalism.

So, I think, there is no such thing as new journalism. It still comes down to good writing, and hard work, and clear thinking. The rest is bullshit. The best motto for all of us is still the last line of James Baldwin's introduction to *Notes of a Native Son:*

"I want to be an honest man and a good writer."

Amen.

May 18, 1972